English Grammar for Students of German

The Study Guide for Those Learning German

Seventh Edition

Cecile Zorach
Franklin and Marshall College

Adam Oberlin
Princeton University

The Olivia and Hill Press®

THE O&H STUDY GUIDES

Jacqueline Morton, editor

English Grammar for Students of Spanish
English Grammar for Students of French
English Grammar for Students of German
English Grammar for Students of Italian
English Grammar for Students of Latin
English Grammar for Students of Russian
English Grammar for Students of Japanese
English Grammar for Students of Arabic
English Grammar for Students of Chinese
Gramática española para estudiantes de inglés

Printed in the U.S.A.

ISBN: 978-0-934034-5-55

Library of Congress Control Number: 2021918262

CONTENTS

LET'S GET STARTED

English Grammar for Students of German (EGSG) explains the grammatical terms that are in your textbook and shows how they relate to English grammar. Once you understand how the terms and concepts apply to English, it will be easier for you to understand and learn German grammar.

Each short chapter is divided into two sections, *In English* and *In German*. Both explain the same grammar point and alert you to the similarities and differences between the two languages. You will also find step-by-step tools to apply grammar rules and to get from an English structure to a German structure. To help you be an efficient language learner, we offer specific study tips for learning different types of words. You can assess your comprehension of the content by doing the Reviews (the answer key is at the end of the book).

EGSG is a supplementary text which can be used with any German textbook or method. To help you customize EGSG to your syllabus and learn which pages to read in preparation for a lesson, you can download correlations to popular 1st year German college textbooks from our website www.oliviahill.com. If you're working with course material developed by your faculty, the detailed index of EGSG makes it easy to correlate it to any topic.

Note: In keeping with our approach to introduce grammar from the perspective of the language of today's students, our examples are based on contemporary spoken English. The more formal written English equivalent is also given to facilitate the transition to German.

TIPS FOR LEARNING GRAMMAR

Grammar is one of the tools you need to communicate orally and in writing. Grammar rules are very useful because they enable a speaker to move from the particular to the general. For instance, the grammar rule to put an "s" when there is more than one object (book vs. books) enables us to apply that to other words (table vs. tables). Without rules, we'd be forced to memorize every word separately.

1. Reading a grammar rule in your textbook is not sufficient. Make sure that you understand the explanation. Studying the examples to see how they illustrate the rule is as important as understanding the rule itself. If anything is not clear, be sure to ask the teacher at the first opportunity. Clear up problems as early as possible so that you don't fall behind.
2. As you progress in your studies, review previous lessons regularly. To facilitate learning, textbooks tend to focus on one grammar point per section. Bear in mind that these points are not independent; they are part of a whole. In other words, as you learn new rules, don't forget the ones you learned before.

3. Repetitive use of grammar rules in different contexts will help you understand how they are applied and to recognize patterns. It will help you to view language not just as a set of rules but as a system of patterns used by people to communicate with one another.

TIPS FOR LEARNING VOCABULARY

One aspect of language learning is remembering many unfamiliar words.

To learn vocabulary — Flashcards are a good, handy tool for learning new words and their meaning. You can carry them with you, group them as you wish, and add information as you advance. Creating your own flashcards is an important first step in learning vocabulary.

1. Write the German word or expression on one side of an index card and its English equivalent on the other side.
2. On the German side add a short sentence using the word or expression. To make sure that your sentence is grammatically correct, copy an example from your textbook substituting the names of people and places with ones you know. It will be easier for you to remember a word in a familiar context. For review purposes, note down the page number of your textbook where the word is introduced.
3. On the German side include any irregularities and whatever information is relevant to the word in question. You will find specific suggestions under the *Study Tips* sections.

How to use the cards – Regardless of the side you're working on, always say the German word out loud.

1. Look at the German side first. Going from German to English is easier than from English to German because it only requires you to recognize the German word. Read the German word(s) out loud, giving the English equivalent, then check your answer on the English side.
2. When you go easily from German to English, turn the cards to the English side. Going from English to German is harder than going from German to English because you have to pull the word and its spelling out of your memory. Say the German equivalent out loud as you write it down, then check the spelling. Some students prefer closing their eyes and visualizing the German word and its spelling.
3. As you progress, put aside the cards you know and concentrate on the ones you still don't know.

How to remember words — Below are suggestions to help you associate a German word with an English word with a similar meaning. This is the first step and it will put the German word in your short-term memory. Use and practice, the next step, will put the words in your long-term memory.

1. Sometimes words are easy to learn because they are similar in English and German. These words are easy to recognize in German, but you will have to concentrate on the differences in spelling and pronunciation.

address	Adresse
to swim	schwimmen
green	grün

One reason they are similar is because of a system of vowel changes that marks different word forms in Germanic languages. Because German and English are both Germanic languages, learning about this system can help you in two ways: 1. to organize and memorize verb forms (p. 52) and 2. to learn new vocabulary by association.

Look at the English and German words below and you will see that each row shows a pattern of vowels across the different types of words.

English			
s**i**ng	s**a**ng	s**u**ng	the s**o**ng
gr**ow**	gr**ew**	gr**ow**n	the gr**ow**th
gr**i**nd	gr**ou**nd	gr**ou**nd	the gr**ou**nds
r**i**de	r**o**de	r**i**dden	the r**i**de

German			
schr**ei**ten	schr**i**tt	geschr**i**tten *(to stride)*	der Schr**i**tt *(the step)*
b**ie**ten	b**o**t	geb**o**ten *(to offer)*	das Geb**o**t *(the offer)*
h**e**lfen	h**a**lf	geh**o**lfen *(to help)*	die H**i**lfe *(the help)*
gew**i**nnen	gew**a**nn	gew**o**nnen *(to win)*	der Gew**i**nn *(the prize)*

You'll learn more about these similarities in advanced German courses.

2. Try to associate the German word with another German word that you already know.

Freund	freundlich	*friend, friendly*
abfahren	Abfahrt	*to depart, departure*
klein	verkleinern	*small, to reduce*

3. If the German word has no similarities to English, rely on any association that is meaningful to you. Different types of associations work for different people. Find the one that works best for you. Here are some suggestions:

- Group words by topics — It is easier to learn new words if you group them according to themes such as food, clothing, sports, school, home, etc. Think about the different kinds of words you will need to communicate about a particular topic. Try to learn action and descriptive words along with the words for people, places, and things. For example, take the topic of your living situation. To create sentences, you need to know more than the words for furniture!

apartment	to rent	cheap, expensive
dorm	to live	clean, dirty
roommate	to share	friendly, nice

- You may also find it helpful to group words by category, such as opposites (big ≠ small, tall ≠ short).

4. To reinforce the German word and its spelling use it in a short sentence.

5. As you encounter words that look and sound alike in both languages but have different meanings, keep a list of these **falsche Freunde** *(false friends* or *false cognates)*.

das Gift	*poison*
eventuell	*possible, potential*
aktuell	*current*

TIPS FOR LEARNING WORD FORMS

Another aspect of language learning is remembering the various forms a word can take; for example, another form of *book* is *books* and *do* can take the form of *does* and *did*. As a general rule, the first part of the word indicates its meaning and the second part indicates its form.

To learn forms — Paper and pencil are the best tools to learn the various forms of a word. You should write them down until you get them right. The following steps will make learning forms easier.

1. Look for a pattern in the different forms of a word.
   - Which letters, if any, remain constant?
   - Which letters change?
   - Is there a pattern to the changes?
   - Is this pattern the same as one you already know?
   - If this pattern is similar to one you already know, what are the similarities and differences?

   We will help you establish patterns in the *Study Tips* following selected chapters.

2. Once you have established the pattern, it will be easy to memorize the forms.
   - Take a blank piece of paper and write down the forms while saying them out loud.
   - Continue until you are able to write all the forms correctly without referring to your textbook.
3. Write short sentences using the various forms.

You will find suggestions on what to write on the cards under the *Study Tips* at the end of the chapter.

TIPS FOR EFFECTIVE STUDY

Before class — Study the sections in EGSG listed in the *German correlations* that correspond to the assigned grammar topic. (If your textbook is not listed, refer to the detailed index for guidance.) You will learn the relevant grammatical terminology, the similarities and differences between English and German, and how to avoid common pitfalls. Afterwards move on to your textbook. Take notes as you study; highlighting is not sufficient. The more often you write down and use vocabulary and rules, the easier it will be for you to remember them. Good preparation enables you to take advantage of classroom activities.

In class — Take notes. This will remind you what the teacher considers important and will reinforce what you are studying. When your teacher gives you a new example or you hear a phrase while watching a video program, write it down so that you can analyze it. Once you have mastered a new concept, make up simple statements. Begin by modeling your sentences after the examples in your textbook. Later you will be able to express your own ideas.

Homework — Complete exercises and activities over several short periods of time rather than in one long session. Don't get behind. You need time to absorb the material and to develop the skills.

Written exercises — As you write German words or sentences, say them out loud. Each time you write, read, say, and hear a word it reinforces it in your memory.

Objective — Your aim is to be able to communicate correctly in German, orally and in writing, without reference to a textbook or dictionary. The study tips throughout this handbook will help you with this learning process.

CAREFUL – Apps, computer programs, audio courses, online videos, etc. can be effective aids to learning outside of class, but only in addition to the study tips outlined above. Repeating words out loud and using pencil and paper are still the best learning tools.

1 WHAT'S IN A WORD?

When you learn another language, in this case German, you must look at each word in four ways: **MEANING, PART OF SPEECH, FUNCTION**, and **FORM**.

1.1 MEANING

An English word may be connected to a German word that has a similar meaning.

> *Tree* has the same meaning as the German word **Baum.**

Words with equivalent meanings are learned by memorizing vocabulary (p. 2). There are many words, called **COGNATES**, that have the same meaning and approximately the same spelling in English and German.

Haus	*house*
Garten	*garden*
Student	*student*
intelligent	*intelligent*

Occasionally knowing one German word will help you learn another.

> Knowing that **Kellner** means *waiter* should help you learn that **Kellnerin** is *waitress*; or knowing that **wohnen** means *to live* and that **Zimmer** means *room* should help you learn that **Wohnzimmer** means *living room*.

However, there is usually little similarity between words and knowing one German word will not help you learn another. In general, you must memorize each vocabulary item separately.

> Knowing that **Mann** means *man* will not help you learn that **Frau** means *woman*.

Words that have the same basic meaning in English and German rarely have identical meanings in all situations.

> The word **Mann** generally has the same meaning as *man*, but it can also mean *husband*. The word **Frau** usually means *woman*, but it can also mean *wife*, a married woman, *Mrs.* or *Ms.*

In addition, every language has its own phrases or way of expressing ideas; these are called **IDIOMATIC EXPRESSIONS** or **IDIOMS**.

> The expression *keep your fingers crossed* must be considered as a whole to be understood, not as individual words: *keep* + *fingers* + *crossed*. The equivalent German expression, **die Daumen drücken** (word-for-word: *press your thumbs*), must also be considered as a whole.

In both English and German there are set combinations of words to convey a meaning. For instance, in English the verb "take" is used in the expression "to take a course". Whereas in German, the verb **belegen** *(to attend)* is used to convey the same meaning.

You will have to be on the alert for these idioms and word combinations because they cannot be translated word-for-word.

1.2 PART OF SPEECH

In English and German a word can be classified as belonging to one of eight categories called **PARTS OF SPEECH.**

noun	article
pronoun	adverb
verb	preposition
adjective	conjunction

Some parts of speech are further broken down according to type. Adjectives, for instance, can be descriptive, interrogative, demonstrative, or possessive. Each part of speech has its own rules for spelling, pronunciation, and use.

In order to choose the correct German equivalent of an English word, you must learn to identify its part of speech. For example, look at the word *plays* in the following sentences.

Axel *plays* soccer.
verb → **spielt**

Axel likes *plays*.
noun → **Schauspiele**

The English word is the same in both sentences. In German, however, different words are used, and different sets of rules apply, because each *plays* belongs to a different part of speech. The various sections of this handbook show you how to identify parts of speech so that you can choose the correct German words and the rules that apply to them.

1.3 FUNCTION

In English and German the role a word plays in a sentence is called its **FUNCTION.** Depending on the sentence, the same word can have a variety of functions.

subject
direct object
indirect object
object of a preposition

In order to choose the correct German equivalent of an English word, you must learn to identify its function. For example, look at the word *her* in the following sentences.

I don't know *her.*
direct object → **sie**

Have you told *her* your story?
indirect object → **ihr**

The English word is the same in both sentences. In German, however, different words are used, and different sets of rules apply, because each *her* has a different function. The various sections of this handbook show you how to identify the function of words so that you can choose the proper German words and the rules that apply to them.

1.4 FORM

In English and in German, a word can influence the form of another word, that is, its spelling and pronunciation. This "matching" is called **AGREEMENT** and it is said that one word "agrees" with another.

I am	*am* agrees with *I*
she is	*is* agrees with *she*

Agreement does not play a big role in English, but it is an important part of the German language. For example, look at the sentences below where the lines indicate which words must agree with one another.

The blue **book** *is on the big old* ***table.***

Das blaue **Buch** ist auf dem großen alten **Tisch.**

In English, the only word that affects another word in the sentence is *book*, which causes us to say *is*. If the word were *books,* we would have to say *are.* In German, the word for *book* **(Buch)** not only affects the word for *is* **(ist)**, but also the spelling and pronunciation of the German words for *the* **(das)** and *blue* **(blaue)**. The words for *is on* **(ist auf)** and *table* **(Tisch)** affect the spelling and pronunciation of the equivalent words for *the* **(dem)**, *big* **(großen)**, and *old* **(alten)**. The only word not affected by the words surrounding it is the word for *on* **(auf)**.

As the various parts of speech are introduced in this handbook, we will go over "agreement" so that you learn which words agree with others and how the agreement is shown.

WHAT IS A NOUN? 2

A **NOUN** is a word that names a person, animal, place, thing, event, or idea. A noun that names a specific person, place, or thing, etc. is called a **PROPER NOUN.** A noun that does not name a specific person, place, or thing, etc. is called a **COMMON NOUN.**

Ingrid is my friend.
(Ingrid: proper noun; friend: common noun)

- a person — Jacob, Katie, Professor Meyer, friend, sister, student, gardener, doctor
- an animal — Snoopy, Fluffy, Mickey Mouse, dog, falcon, fish, bear
- a place — Zurich, Bavaria, New York, Austria, Europe, stadium, restaurant, city, state, country
- a thing — Monday, White House, Volkswagen, desk, house, border, water, hand
- an event or activity — the Olympics, Thanksgiving, birth, graduation, jogging, growth
- an idea or concept — Stalinism, Murphy's Law, Game Theory, truth, poverty, peace, fear, beauty, time, humor, justice, hatred

As you can see, a noun is not only a word that names something that is tangible (i.e., something you can touch), such as *desk, restaurant*, or *White House*, it can also be the name of something that is abstract (i.e., that you cannot touch), such as *truth, peace,* and *humor.*

A noun made up of two or more words is called a **COMPOUND NOUN**. A compound noun may be made up of two common nouns written as one word *(snowball)*, as two words *(school year)*, or with a hyphen *(self-interest)*. It can also be a combination of a common noun and other parts of speech such as *Berlin Wall* [Berlin = proper noun, wall = common noun]. Depending on usage the same form of a noun can be used as a proper or common noun. You can distinguish one from the other because the noun is capitalized when it is a proper noun and not capitalized when it is a common noun, i.e. the *Civil War* as opposed to a *civil war*.

2.1 IN ENGLISH

Proper nouns always begin with a capital letter. Common nouns, however, only begin with a capital letter when they are the first word of a sentence or question.

To help you learn to recognize nouns, look at the paragraph below where the nouns are in italics.

> The ***United States*** imports many ***items*** from German-speaking ***countries.*** German ***automobiles,*** ranging from moderately priced ***models*** to elegant ***cars,*** have earned a ***reputation*** here for their excellent ***performance. Germany*** also supplies us with fine ***tools, cameras,*** and ***electronics.*** Many ***Americans*** value ***watches*** imported from ***Switzerland***. Nearly everyone in our ***country*** appreciates the ***taste*** of Swiss ***chocolate.***

2.2 IN GERMAN

Nouns are very easy to recognize in German since all nouns, proper and common, are capitalized, regardless of where they are in a sentence. However, it makes it harder to tell common nouns apart from proper nouns, so do pay attention to context clues such as the German equivalents of *the* or *a*, which precede common nouns or obvious names of people or places which are proper nouns.

German has many compound nouns which are written as one word and may contain two or more common nouns. For example, **das Geburtstagsgeschenk** *(the birthday gift)* consists of the noun **der Geburtstag** *(the birthday)* and **das Geschenk** *(the gift)*. In compound nouns, the final noun determines both the grammatical gender and the plural form of the entire compound noun (Gender, p. 20; Number, p. 16).

2.3 TERMS USED TO TALK ABOUT NOUNS

- **CASE** — In German, a noun can have a variety of forms depending on its function in the sentence (Case, p. 32).
- **GENDER** – In German, a noun has a gender; that is, it can be classified according to whether it is masculine, feminine, or neuter (Gender, p. 21).
- **NUMBER** – A noun has number; that is, it can be identified as being singular or plural (Number, p. 16).
- **FUNCTION** – A noun can have a variety of functions in a sentence; that is, it can be the subject of the sentence (Subject, p. 45), a predicate noun (Predicates, p. 48), or an object (Objects, p. 63).

REVIEW ACTIVITY

Circle the common nouns and underline the proper nouns in the following sentences:

a. Katie asks her teacher many questions about Europe.

b. Mrs. Schneider answers her students with patience.

c. Curiosity is an important part of learning.

d. Katie and her classmates hear stories about Berlin, the capital of Germany.

e. The class tours an exhibit about German settlers.

f. German is spoken in several countries, including in parts of Luxembourg.

WHAT ARE PREFIXES AND SUFFIXES? 3

A **PREFIX** consists of one or more syllables added to the beginning of a word to change that word's meaning.

nuclear	→	*anti*nuclear
approve	→	*dis*approve
negotiate	→	*re*negotiate

A **SUFFIX** consists of one or more syllables added to the end of a word to change that word into a different part of speech (Word, p. 7).

gentle (adjective)	→	gentle*ness* (noun)
love (noun)	→	lov*able* (adjective)
establish (verb)	→	establish*ment* (noun)
deep (adjective)	→	dep*th* (noun)

To see how prefixes and suffixes work, look at the various English words that come from the Latin verb **duco** *(to lead)*. Different prefixes give us verbs such as *in*duce, *re*duce, *se*duce, *pro*duce, and *intro*duce. Added suffixes result in different parts of speech, for example: induc*tion* (noun), induc*tive* (adjective), induc*tively* (adverb).

3.1 IN ENGLISH

Many English prefixes and suffixes come from Latin and Greek, and some are of native Germanic origin. A good English dictionary will tell you the meaning and function of the various prefixes and suffixes.

Knowing English suffixes can help you identify the parts of speech in a sentence and increase your English vocabulary.

-able, -ible	toler*able*	→	adjective
-ly	quick*ly*	→	adverb
-ence, -ance	reli*ance*	→	noun

NOUNS FORMED WITH PREFIXES (Nouns, p. 9)

By adding a prefix to an existing noun, you can form a new noun with a different meaning.

anti- (against)	+ body	→	*anti*body
sub- (under)	+ marine	→	*sub*marine
mal- (bad)	+ nutrition	→	*mal*nutrition

VERBS FORMED WITH PREFIXES (Verbs, p. 29).

A new verb with a different meaning can be formed by adding a prefix to an existing verb.

> He *used* the tool correctly.
> (*used* = verb)
>
> He *mis*used the tool, and it broke.
> (*misused* = verb)

A verb can also be formed by adding a prefix to another part of speech.

> Anja is my new *friend*.
> (*friend* = noun)
>
> She *be*friended me on my first day at the new school.
> (*befriended* = verb)

3.2 IN GERMAN

As in English, prefixes and suffixes can be used to change the meaning of words and to change a word's part of speech.

NOUNS FORMED WITH SUFFIXES

Certain suffixes not only affect the meaning of a noun but also determine the gender of the noun being formed (Gender, p. 20).

- noun + **-chen** and **-lein** → new noun is neuter
  These suffixes show that the noun is a diminutive, i.e., something reduced in size.

Noun		New noun neuter	
das Brot (neut.)	*bread*	das Bröt**chen**	*roll, little bread*
der Brief (masc.)	*letter*	das Brief**lein**	*small letter*
die Kerze (fem.)	*candle*	das Kerz**lein**	*little candle*

- adjective + **-heit, -keit, -ung, -nis,** etc. → feminine noun
  These suffixes turn an adjective into a noun expressing an abstract quality (p. 116).

Adjective		Feminine noun	
schön	*beautiful*	die Schön**heit**	*beauty*
frei	*free*	die Frei**heit**	*freedom*
möglich	*possible*	die Möglich**keit**	*possibility*
finster	*dark*	die Finster**nis**	*darkness*
beobachten	*to observe*	die Beobacht**ung**	*observation*

VERBS FORMED WITH PREFIXES

The infinitive form of a verb is always one word, i.e., the prefix is part of the verb: **ausgehen** *(to go out)*, **besuchen** *(to visit)*. However, that is not always the case when the verb is conjugated (Conjugation, p. 50). Prefixes are divided into two groups depending on whether or not they can be separated from the verb.

- **SEPARABLE PREFIXES** – German verbs with separable prefixes are similar to English verbs that are regularly used with a preposition (Prepositions, p. 74); namely, they are separate words functioning as a unit with the verb.

  They *are going out* tonight at 7:00 P.M.
  (out = preposition)

  He *picks up* his friend after class.
  (up = preposition)

  Separable prefixes in German include the following: **ab-, an-, auf-, aus-, bei-, ein-, fort-, her-, hin-, mit-, nach-, vor-, weg-, weiter-, zurück-, zusammen-.** Let us look at two examples to see how these prefixes can be separated from the verb.

Infinitive	Sentence
ausgehen *(to go out)*	Hans und ich **gehen** morgen **aus.** *Hans and I **are going out** tomorrow.*
ankommen *(to arrive)*	Der Zug **kommt** heute spät **an.** *The train **is arriving** late today.*

- **INSEPARABLE PREFIXES** – German verbs with inseparable prefixes function as one word since these prefixes are never separated from the basic verb. Inseparable prefixes in German include the following: **be-, emp-, ent-, er-, ge-, miss-, ver-, zer-.** Let us look at two examples.

Infinitive	Sentence
besuchen *(to visit)*	Wir **besuchen** unsere Tante. *We **are visiting** our aunt.*
vergessen *(to forget)*	Du **vergißt** immer dein Buch. *You always **forget** your book.*

Some prefixes, such as **durch-, über-, um-,** and **unter-,** can be either separable or inseparable depending on usage. Your German textbook will explain the rules for using verbs with separable and inseparable prefixes. When you learn a new verb formed with a prefix, memorize whether the prefix is separable or not.

STUDY TIPS
PREFIXES AND SUFFIXES

Flashcards

① Create flashcards of German verbal prefixes ***(an-, mit-, ver-, ent-, etc.)***. On the back of the card, write "Sep" (separable) or "Insep" (inseparable). If the prefix is easily translated, add the English translation. Underneath, write an example word using that prefix. If the verb has a separable prefix, add a short example sentence to illustrate the separation.

mit-	Sep; *with* mitkommen *(to come along)*
ver-	Insep verstehen *(to understand)*

Some textbooks use a period to distinguish separable prefixes from inseparable prefixes.

an.kommen *(to arrive)*	- separable
bekommen *(to receive)*	- inseparable

② Create another set of flashcards. On the German side, write the infinitive of the verb stem at the top of the card. Underneath it, make two columns: one for the verb stem with separable prefixes, the other for the verb stem with inseparable prefixes. On the back, using the same layout, write the English translations.

Verb stem: stehen *to stand*

Sep. prefix	**Insep. prefix**
aufstehen *to stand up*	bestehen *to pass a test*
anstehen *to stand in line*	verstehen *to understand*

Practice

① Learn the meaning of the verb stem by flipping the cards first on the German side and then on the English side.

② Learn the meaning of the verbs with prefixes by flipping cards as under #1. Occasionally, the meaning of the prefixes will give you a clue as to the change of meaning of the verb stem.

③ Do the above exercises orally as the verb forms with separable prefixes are pronounced differently from those with inseparable prefixes: if the prefix is separable, it is the stressed part of the verb form (**auf**stehen) , if the prefix is inseparable, it is the verb stem that is the stressed part of the verb form (ver**stehen**).

REVIEW ACTIVITY

I. Underline the prefixes in the following words.

a. decode

b. enlarge

c. misunderstand

d. recover

e. preserve

f. performance

II. Underline the suffixes in the following words.

a. dependency

b. graceful

c. sleepless

d. exquisitely

e. happiness

f. questionable

4 WHAT IS MEANT BY NUMBER?

NUMBER in the grammatical sense means that a word can be classified as singular or plural. When a word refers to one person or thing, it is said to be **SINGULAR**; when it refers to more than one, it is **PLURAL**.

one *book* (singular)	two *books* (plural)

More parts of speech indicate number in German than in English, and there are also more spelling and pronunciation changes in German than in English.

English	**German**
nouns	nouns
verbs	verbs
pronouns	pronouns
demonstrative adjectives	all adjectives
	articles

Since each part of speech (p. 7) follows its own rules to indicate number, you will find number discussed in the sections dealing with articles, the various types of adjectives and pronouns, as well as in all sections on verbs. In this section we will look at number only as it is reflected in nouns.

4.1 IN ENGLISH

A singular noun is made plural in one of two ways.

- a singular noun can add an "-s" or "-es"

book	book*s*
kiss	kiss*es*

- a singular noun can change its spelling

man	m*e*n
leaf	lea*ves*
child	child*ren*

Some nouns, called **COLLECTIVE NOUNS**, refer to a group of persons or things, but the noun itself is considered singular.

> A soccer *team* has eleven players.
> My *family* is well.

4.2 IN GERMAN

As in English, the plural form of German nouns is often spelled differently, and therefore pronounced differently, from the singular form. German plurals, however, are less predictable than English plurals; there are more endings and more internal spelling changes than in English. As you learn new nouns in German, you should memorize each noun's gender (p. 20) and its singular and plural forms. In the examples below, notice that besides adding different endings German often uses an **umlaut (¨)** to form plural nouns.

- singular noun + **-n** or **-en**

Auge	Auge**n**	*eye*	*eyes*
Frau	Frau**en**	*woman*	*women*

- singular noun + **-e** (**umlaut** is sometimes added)

das Bein	die Bein**e**	*leg*	*legs*
der Stuhl	die St**ü**hl**e**	*chair*	*chairs*

- singular noun + **-er** (**umlaut** added when the stem vowel is **a, o, u,** or **au**)

das Buch	die B**ü**ch**er**	*book*	*books*
das Haus	die H**ä**us**er**	*house*	*houses*

- singular noun + no ending (**umlaut** added when the stem vowel is **a, o, u,** or **au)**

der Lehrer	die Lehrer	*teacher*	*teachers*
der Vater	die V**ä**ter	*father*	*fathers*

For the plural of compound nouns see page 10.

STUDY TIPS
NOUNS AND THEIR NUMBER

Flashcards

Sort out the flashcards for nouns and add the plural form of the noun, preceded by the definite article (Articles, p. 25).

Patterns

Learning the plural forms of German nouns will be easier if you can determine some patterns.

(1) Create a short list of nouns that have the same ending in the singular. Write down the plural form beside each noun.

Group 1		**Group 2**	
Prüf**ung**	Prüfung**en**	Wint**er**	Winter
Wohn**ung**	Wohnung**en**	Zimm**er**	Zimmer
Zeit**ung**	Zeitung**en**	Lehr**er**	Lehrer

What pattern do you see?
- nouns ending in **–ung** add **–en** in the plural (Group 1)
- nouns ending in **–er** do not change in the plural (Group 2)

(2) Try to determine some patterns of number based on the gender of the noun. Create lists of feminine and masculine nouns. Write the plural form beside each noun.

Feminine	**Plural**
Schule	Schul**en**
Tür	Tür**en**
Freiheit	Freiheit**en**
Spezialität	Spezialität**en**
Freundschaft	Freundschaft**en**

Masculine	**Plural**
Lehrer	Lehrer
Freund	Freund**e**
Bruder	Br**ü**der

Neuter	**Plural**
Märchen	Märchen
Pferd	Pferd**e**
Wort	Wört**er**
Bett	Bett**en**

What pattern do you see?

- feminine nouns (and some neuter nouns) often use –**n** or –**en** to form the plural.
- feminine nouns formed with suffixes, **-keit, –heit, -tät,** and –**schaft** use –**en** to form the plural.
- neuter nouns with diminutive suffixes, **-chen** and **-lein**, do not add any ending in the plural.
- some masculine and neuter nouns do not add any ending in the plural.
- masculine nouns often use an umlaut and/or an **-e** to form the plural.
- neuter nouns often use an umlaut and/or an **-er** to form the plural.

(3) Paying attention to the ending of a German noun will provide you with clues to both its gender and how to form its plural. The plural form of one noun can help you remember the plural form of another noun with the same ending.

REVIEW ACTIVITY

I. Circle the English words that are in the plural.

a. pencils
b. suitcase
c. business
d. feet
e. group
f. family
g. goose
h. women

II. Under the Plural column, circle the parts of the German word that indicate the plural form.

Singular	**Plural**
a. Wort	Wörter
b. Stuhl	Stühle
c. Kind	Kinder
d. Studentin	Studentinnen
e. Auto	Autos
f. Mangel	Mängel
g. Frau	Frauen
h. Messer	Messer

5 WHAT IS MEANT BY GENDER?

GENDER in the grammatical sense means that a word can be classified as **MASCULINE**, **FEMININE**, or **NEUTER**.

> Did Franz give Ingrid the book? Yes, he gave it to her.
> he = masc., it = neuter, her = fem.

Grammatical gender is not very important in English. However, it is at the very heart of the German language, where the gender of a word is often reflected not only in the word itself, but also in the way all the words connected to it are spelled and pronounced.

More parts of speech indicate gender in German than in English.

English	**German**
pronouns	nouns
possessive adjectives	articles
	pronouns
	all adjectives

Since each part of speech follows its own rules to indicate gender, you will find gender discussed in the sections dealing with articles and with the various types of pronouns and adjectives. In this section we shall only look at the gender of nouns (Nouns, p. 9).

5.1 IN ENGLISH

Nouns themselves do not have gender, but sometimes their meaning indicates a gender based on the biological sex of the person or animal the noun represents. For example, when we replace a proper or common noun that refers to one man or woman, we use *he* for male identifying people (henceforth referred to as "male") and *she* for female identifying people (henceforth referred to as "female").

- nouns and pronouns referring to males indicate the **MASCULINE** gender

> Lukas came home; he was happy; the dog was glad to see him.
> Lukas = noun (male), he = masculine, him = masculine

- nouns and pronouns referring to females indicate the **FEMININE** gender

> Anja came home; she was happy; the dog was glad to see her.
> Anja = noun (female), she = feminine, her = feminine

All the proper or common nouns that are not perceived as having a biological gender are considered **NEUTER** and are replaced by *it* when they refer to one thing, place, or idea.

> The city of Munich is lovely. I enjoyed visiting it.
> city = noun, it = neuter

5.2 IN GERMAN

All nouns—common nouns and proper nouns—have a gender; they are masculine, feminine, or neuter. Do not confuse the grammatical terms "masculine" and "feminine" with the terms "male" and "female" which apply to persons or animals.

Here are some examples of English nouns classified under the gender of their German equivalent.

Masculine	**Feminine**	**Neuter**
table	lamp	window
heaven	hope	girl
state	Switzerland	Germany
beginning	reality	topic

Textbooks and dictionaries usually indicate the gender of a noun with *m.* for masculine, *f.* for feminine, or *n.* for neuter. Sometimes definite articles are used: **der** for masculine, **die** for feminine, or **das** for neuter (Articles, p. 25).

A German noun will usually have different forms when it refers to the different sexes. For example, the noun *student* has two equivalents, a feminine form **Studentin** for females and a masculine form **Student** for males. However, consistent with the modern trend toward gender-neutral terminology, students are usually referred to with the neutral **Studierende**.

As you learn a new noun, you should always learn its gender because it will affect the form of the words related to it.

CAREFUL – Do not rely on biological gender to indicate the grammatical gender of German nouns that can refer to either a male or a female person. For instance, the grammatical gender of the nouns **Kind** *(child)* and **Baby** *(baby)* is always neuter. Likewise, **Mädchen** *(girl)* is always neuter, even though it always refers to a female.

STUDY TIPS
NOUNS AND THEIR GENDER

Flashcards

1. Make a flashcard for each noun. You can do this by hand, or use a free online tool (simply search for "flash card maker"). Most online tools allow you to type in the information, practice with the cards online, and/or print out paper cards. For those with access to an Apple computer, consider making flashcards using Provoc (www.arizona-software.ch/provoc). This free software allows you to move your flashcards onto an iPod for vocabulary practice on the go!
2. Use either colored paper or a highlighter to color code the flashcards based on the gender of the noun: masculine = blue, feminine = red, neuter = green. Associating the noun with blue, red, or green will help you remember its gender.
3. On one side, write the German noun, including the singular article (Articles, p. 25). On the other side, write the word in English or use an image to depict the noun. You can find small images online at The Internet Picture Dictionary (www.pdictionary.com/german), or photos of objects in a German setting at the Culturally Authentic Pictorial Lexicon (www.washjeff.edu/CAPL).

Pattern

Gender can sometimes be determined by looking at the ending of the German noun. Here are some common endings you will want to notice.

Masculine endings

- all nouns referring to male persons that end in **-er, -ist, -ling, -ent**

der Physiker	*the physicist*
der Pianist	*the pianist*
der Jüngling	*the young man*
der Student	*the student*

- names of seasons (except **das Frühjahr,** *spring*), months, days, parts of days (except **die Nacht,** *night*), geographical directions, and weather phenomena

der Sommer	*summer*
der Januar	*January*
der Montag	*Monday*
der Mittag	*noon*
der Wind	*the wind*
der Westen	*west*

- most nouns which end in **-ig, -or, -ismus, -pf, -f, -ast, -ich**

der Pfennig	*the penny*
der Doktor	*the doctor*
der Optimismus	*optimism*
der Kopf	*the head*
der Senf	*mustard*
der Palast	*the palace*
der Teppich	*the carpet, the rug*

Feminine endings

- most two-syllable nouns which end in **-e**

die Lampe	*the lamp*
die Seife	*the soap*

Common exceptions: **der Name,** *the name,* **der Käse,** *the cheese,* which are masculine, and **das Auge,** *the eye,* which is neuter.

- all nouns referring to female persons which end in **-in**

die Studentin	*the student*
die Professorin	*the Professor*

- all nouns ending in **-ei, -ie, -heit, -keit, -schaft, -ung, -ion, -tät, -ur, -ik, -a**

die Bücherei	*library*
die Drogerie	*drugstore*
die Dummheit	*stupidity*
die Möglichkeit	*possibility*
die Freundschaft	*friendship*
die Prüfung	*test*
die Reaktion	*reaction*
die Universität	*university*
die Natur	*nature*
die Musik	*music*
die Pizza	*pizza*

Neuter endings

- all nouns ending in **-klein** or **-chen**

das Glöcklein	*the little bell*
das Brötchen	*the bread roll*

- all nouns ending in **-um, -ium or -tum**

das Studium	*study*
das Aluminium	*aluminum*
das Visum	*the visa*
das Eigentum	*property*
das Christentum	*Christianity*

- most nouns beginning with **Ge-**
  das Gebäude — *the building*
  das Gebet — *the prayer*
  das Gelächter — *laughter*

Common exceptions: **der Gedanke,** *the thought,* **der Geruch,** *the scent,* which are masculine, and **die Gebühr,** *the fee,* **die Gefahr,** *the danger,* which are feminine.

- verb infinitives used as nouns (Gerund, p. 109)
  das Lesen — *reading*
  das Singen — *singing*

REVIEW ACTIVITY

By consulting the lists in the Study Tips above determine the gender of the following German words: masculine (M), feminine (F), or neuter (N).

a.	Lehrer *(teacher)*	M	F	N
b.	Brötchen *(bread roll)*	M	F	N
c.	Freundin *(friend)*	M	F	N
d.	Sonntag *(Sunday)*	M	F	N
e.	Buhhandlung *(bookstore)*	M	F	N
f.	Fotoalbum *(photo album)*	M	F	N
g.	Freiheit *(freedom)*	M	F	N
h.	Käfig *(cage)*	M	F	N

WHAT IS AN ARTICLE? 6

An **ARTICLE** is a word placed before a noun to show whether the noun refers to a specific person, animal, place, thing, event, or idea, or whether the noun refers to an unspecified person, thing, or idea.

> I saw *the* video you spoke about.
> a specific video
>
> I saw *a* video at school.
> an unspecified video

In English and in German, there are two types of articles, definite articles and indefinite articles.

6.1 DEFINITE ARTICLES

IN ENGLISH

A **DEFINITE ARTICLE** is used before a noun when we are speaking about a particular person, place, animal, thing, event, or idea. There is one definite article, *the.*

> I read *the* book you recommended.
> a specific book
>
> Did you pass *the* exam?
> a specific exam

The definite article remains *the* when the noun that follows becomes plural.

> I read *the books* you recommended.

IN GERMAN

As in English, a definite article is used before a noun when referring to a specific person, place, animal, thing, or idea.

> Hast du **die Klausur** bestanden?
> *Did you pass **the exam?***

In German, the article works hand-in-hand with the noun to which it belongs in that it matches the noun's gender, number, and case. This "matching" is called **AGREEMENT**, one says that "the article *agrees* with the noun" (Gender, p. 20 ; Number, p. 16; Case, p. 32).

A different definite article is used, depending on three factors.

1. **GENDER** – whether the noun is masculine, feminine, or neuter.
2. **NUMBER** – whether the noun is singular or plural.
3. **CASE** – the function of the noun in the sentence.

There are four basic forms of the definite article in the nominative (or subject) case: three singular forms and one plural.

- **der** indicates that the noun is masculine singular
  der Baum ***the*** *tree*
- **die** indicates that the noun is feminine singular
  die Tür ***the*** *door*
- **das** indicates that the noun is neuter singular
  das Haus ***the*** *house*
- **die** is also the definite article for all plural nouns
  die Türen ***the*** *doors*

CAREFUL – Since the same definite article **die** is used with feminine singular nouns and with plural nouns, you will have to rely on other indicators to determine the number of the noun. The most common indicator is the form of the noun itself: is it the singular form or the plural form of the noun?

die **Tür**
the ***door***
Tür is a singular noun; therefore, **die** is feminine singular.

die **Türen**
the ***doors***
Türen is a plural noun; therefore, **die** is plural.

As your study of German progresses, you will discover other indicators to help you identify if the definite article is singular or plural.

6.2 INDEFINITE ARTICLES

IN ENGLISH

An indefinite article is used before a noun when we are speaking about an unspecified person, animal, place, thing, event, or idea. There are two indefinite articles, *a* and *an*.

- *a* is used before a word beginning with a consonant
  I saw a video at school.
  not a specific video
- *an* is used before a word beginning with a vowel or a vowel sound
  I passed an exam.
  not a specific exam

  She is taking an honors class.
  not a specific honors class

IN GERMAN

As in English, an indefinite article is used before a noun when we are not speaking about a specific person, animal, place, thing, event, or idea. Just as German definite articles, indefinite articles must agree with the noun in gender, number, and case. There are two basic forms for the indefinite article in the nominative (or subject) case. As in English, the indefinite article is used only with a singular noun.

- **ein** indicates that the noun is masculine or neuter

  ein Baum (masculine) — *a tree*

  ein Haus (neuter) — *a house*

- **eine** indicates that the noun is feminine

  eine Tür (feminine) — *a door*

Your textbook will instruct you on the different forms of the definite and indefinite articles in greater detail.

STUDY TIPS

NOUNS AND ARTICLES

Flashcards

1. Use your noun flashcards to memorize the meaning of the noun and the correct form of the definite article. As you look at the English side, say the definite article + noun out loud in German.
2. Repeat the above, this time using the plural definite article + the plural form of the noun.
3. Repeat the above, this time using the indefinite article + the singular form of the noun. Add an adjective such as **klein** *(small)* whose ending changes according to whether it precedes a masculine **(der, -er),** feminine **(die, -e),** or neuter **(das, -es)** noun. The change in ending of the adjective will reinforce the noun's gender in your memory.

   ein kleiner Hund (m.) — *a small dog*
   eine kleine Katze (f.) — *a small cat*
   ein kleines Kind (n.) — *a small child*

④ As you learn more about case and other grammatical forms, practice building on these phrases with prepositions or in sentences.

mit einer kleinen Katze	*with a small cat*
Sieht er einen kleinen Hund?	*Does he see a small dog?*

REVIEW ACTIVITY

Below is a list of English nouns preceded by a definite or indefinite article.

Write the corresponding German article for each noun on the line provided. The German dictionary entry indicates whether the noun is masculine (m.), feminine (f.), or neuter (n.).

		Dictionary entry	German article
a.	the book	Buch, n.	______
b.	a table	Tisch, m.	______
c.	a class	Klasse, f.	______
d.	the telephone	Telefon, n.	______
e.	a car	Auto, n.	______
f.	the sister	Schwester, f.	______
g.	the ball	Ball, m.	______
h.	the Independence Day	Unabhängigkeitstag, m.	______

WHAT IS A VERB? 7

A **VERB** is a word that indicates the action of the sentence. The word "action" is used in its broadest sense; it is not necessarily a physical action. Let us look at different types of words that are verbs.

a physical activity	to run, to hit, to talk, to walk
a mental activity	to hope, to believe, to imagine, to dream, to think
a condition	to be, to have, to seem
a change of state	to become, to be born, to die

Many verbs, however, do not fall neatly into one of the above four categories. They are verbs nevertheless because they represent the "action" of the sentence.

The book *costs* only $10.00.
to cost

The table *seats* eight.
to seat

The verb is the most important word in a sentence. You cannot write a **COMPLETE SENTENCE**, that is, express a complete thought, without a verb.

It is important to identify verbs because the function of a word in a sentence often depends on its relationship to the verb. For instance, the subject of a sentence is the word doing the action of the verb and the object is the word receiving the action of the verb (Subject, p. 45 ; Objects, p. 63).

7.1 IN ENGLISH

The basic form of a verb is called the **INFINITIVE**: *(to) eat, (to) sleep, (to) drink*. In the dictionary the infinitive is listed without the "to": *eat, sleep, drink*. When the infinitive is used in a sentence it is always accompanied by another verb that is conjugated (Conjugation, p. 50).

To study *is* challenging.
infinitive conjugated verb

It *is* important *to be* on time.
conjugated verb infinitive

Axel and Jade *want* *to play* tennis.
conjugated verb infinitive

After verbs such as *must, let, should,* and *can,* English uses the dictionary form of the verb without *to*.

Gabi *must* *do* her homework.
dictionary form

The parents *let* the children *open* the presents.
dictionary form

To help you learn to recognize verbs, look at the paragraph below where the verbs are in italics.

> The three students ***entered*** the restaurant, ***selected*** a table, ***hung up*** their coats, and ***sat*** down. They began ***to look*** at the menu and ***asked*** the waitress what she ***recommended.*** She ***named*** the daily special, beef stew. It ***was*** not expensive. The service ***was*** slow, but the food ***tasted*** very good. Good cooking, they ***decided, takes*** time. They ***ate*** pastry for dessert and ***finished*** the meal with coffee.

7.2 IN GERMAN

As in English, verbs play an essential role in a sentence. The infinitive is the form under which verbs are listed in the dictionary; e.g., **arbeiten,** *to work*. (Notice that the English equivalent of a German infinitive is usually preceded by *to*.) Sometimes German infinitives are preceded by **zu (zu arbeiten).** Your textbook will explain when **zu** is necessary. As in English, the infinitive is always used with the conjugated form of another verb.

The infinitive form always ends with the letters **-n** or **-en.**

Axel wants ***to play*** *tennis.*
Axel will Tennis **spielen.**
conjugated verb infinitive

Lukas does not want ***to do*** *that.*
Lukas will das nicht **tun.**
conjugated verb infinitive

Anja tries ***to play*** *something else with Lukas.*
Anja versucht mit Lukas etwas anders **zu spielen.**
Anja tries with Lukas something else to play
conjugated verb infinitive

In the chapters on objects (p. 63) and reflexive verbs (p. 93) you will find several examples of how verbs function differently in German and in English.

7.3 TERMS USED TO TALK ABOUT VERBS

- **INFINITIVE OR DICTIONARY FORM** – The verb form that is the name of the verb is called an infinitive: *(to) eat, (to) sleep, (to) drink.*
- **CONJUGATION** – A verb is conjugated or changes in form to agree with its subject: *I do, he does* (Conjugation, p. 51).
- **TENSE** – A verb indicates tense, that is, the time (present, past, or future) of the action: *I am, I was, I will be* (Tense, p. 59)
- **MOOD** – A verb shows mood, that is, the speaker's perception that what he or she is saying is fact, command, possibility, or wish (Mood, p. 178).
- **VOICE** – A verb shows voice, that is, the relation between the subject and the action of the verb (Voice, p. 188).
- **PARTICIPLE** – A verb may be used to form a participle: *writing, written, singing, sung* (Participles, p. 106).
- **TRANSITIVE OR INTRANSITIVE** – A verb can be classified as transitive or intransitive depending on whether or not the verb can take a direct object (Objects, p. 63).

REVIEW ACTIVITY

I. Circle the verbs in the following sentences.

a. Katie and Jacob meet at the library.

b. The students eat their lunch at school.

c. We stayed home because we expected a phone call.

d. Rachel took a bath, finished her novel, and went to bed.

e. Sam felt better after he talked to his friends.

f. When he drives himself to work, he always arrives early.

II. Write the infinitive form of the verb in the sentences below.

a. We taught them everything they know. ____________________

b. I am tired today. ____________________

c. They had a good time. ____________________

d. She leaves next week for Konstanz. ____________________

e. He swam every day in the summer. ____________________

f. Last weekend Christina found a lost dog. ____________________

8 WHAT IS MEANT BY CASE?

CASE in the grammatical sense means that a different form of the word is used depending on the word's function in the sentence.

> *I* see Axel in class.
> the person speaking
> function → subject
>
> Axel sees *me* in class.
> the person speaking
> function → object

In the sentences above, the person speaking is referred to by the forms "I" and "me." Different forms are used because in each sentence the person speaking has a different grammatical function. In the first sentence, *I* is used because the person speaking is doing the "seeing" and in the second sentence *me* is used because the person speaking is the object of the "seeing."

More parts of speech are affected by case in German than in English.

English	**German**
some pronouns	all pronouns
	nouns
	adjectives
	articles

8.1 FUNCTION OF WORDS

The grammatical role of a word in a sentence is called its **FUNCTION.** The function is often based on the word's relationship to the verb (Verb, 29). Here is a list of the various functions a word can have, with reference to the section in this handbook where each function is studied in detail.

- **SUBJECT** – A noun or pronoun that performs the action of a verb (Subject, p. 45).
- **PREDICATE NOUN** – Pronoun that is linked to the subject by a linking verb (Predicates, p. 48).
- **OBJECT** – A noun or pronoun that is the receiver of the action of a verb (Objects, p. 63). There are different types of objects: direct objects, indirect objects, and objects of a preposition.

To understand the meaning of a sentence, we must identify the function of the various words that make up the sentence. In English, the function of a word is usually indicated by where it is placed in a sentence. In German, where word order changes more often, the function of a word is marked by its case form or that of a word associated with it, such as an article before a noun.

Knowing how to analyze the function of words in an English sentence will help you to establish which case is required in the German sentence.

8.2 IN ENGLISH

English nouns do not change form to indicate different functions (p. 9). For instance, the same form of the noun is used if it is the doer of the action (the subject), the receiver of the direct object (the direct object), or the receiver of the direct object (the indirect object). The function of a noun in a sentence is indicated by where it is placed in the sentence.

We easily recognize the difference in meaning between the following two sentences purely on the basis of word order.

> *The student* gives *the professor* the essay.
> Here the student is giving the essay and the professor is receiving it.
>
> *The professor* gives *the student* the essay.
> Here the professor is giving the essay and the student is receiving it.

These two sentences show how we can change the function of a noun by changing its place in the sentence, and consequently change the meaning of the sentence. As we shall see below, that is not the case with English pronouns.

In English the function of a personal pronoun (Personal pronouns, p. 40) is indicated not only by its place in the sentence, but also by its case. As you can see in the two examples below, both the word order and the form of the pronoun give the sentence meaning.

> *I* know *them.*
> *They* know *me.*

We cannot say, "*I* know *they*" or "*They* know *I*" because the forms "they" and "I" can only be used to refer to the person doing the action. If you learn to recognize the different cases of pronouns in English, it will help you understand the German case system.

English pronouns have three cases.

- **NOMINATIVE CASE** – This case is used when a pronoun is a subject or replaces a predicate nominative.

  > *She* and *I* went to the movies.
  > subjects nominative
  >
  > It was *he* who did the deed.
  > predicate nominative case

- **OBJECTIVE CASE** – This case is used when a pronoun is an object.

  > Axel saw *him.*
  > object objective case
  >
  > Alex sent *them* a note.
  > object objective case

- **POSSESSIVE CASE** – This case is used when a pronoun shows ownership (Possessive pronouns, p. 134).

  Is this book _yours_?
  possessive case

  Julia called her parents, but I wrote _mine_ an e-mail.
  possessive case

8.3 IN GERMAN

Unlike in English where only pronouns change form to indicate case, in German many parts of speech change form depending on the function of the word in the sentence. The case of a German word is sometimes reflected not only by the form of the word itself, but also by the form of the words that accompany it. We have limited the examples in this section to the case of nouns and their accompanying articles.

German has four different cases, and each case reflects a different function of the word in a sentence.

- **NOMINATIVE CASE** – This case is used for the subject of a sentence and for predicate nouns. It is the form of nouns listed in a vocabulary list or a dictionary. This case corresponds to the nominative case in English.
- **ACCUSATIVE CASE** – This case is used for most direct objects and after certain prepositions (Prepositions, p. 74). The accusative and the dative below correspond to the objective case in English.
- **DATIVE CASE** – This case is used primarily for indirect objects, after certain prepositions, and for direct objects after certain verbs. The dative and the accusative above correspond to the objective case in English.
- **GENITIVE CASE** – This case is used to show possession (Possessive, p. 127) or close relation, after certain prepositions, and for direct objects after a handful of verbs. The genitive corresponds to the possessive forms in English.

The case of a noun is most often indicated by the ending of the accompanying article (Articles, p. 25); however, the form of the noun itself can also change. Each case has a singular and plural form (Number, p. 16). The complete set of case forms for any noun and its article is called the noun's **DECLENSION**. When you have memorized these forms, you are able to "decline" that noun.

Case affects the form of masculine and neuter nouns in the genitive singular and of all nouns in the dative plural.

- masculine and neuter singular nouns, genitive singular → add **–(e)s**

Nominative	**Genitive**
Mann (m. sing.)	Mann**es**
Kind (neut. sing.)	Kind**es**
Studium (neut. sing.)	Studium**s**

- all nouns, dative plural → add **–n** (if they don't already end with **–n**)

Nominative	**Dative**
Männer (m. pl.)	Männer**n**
Kinder (neut. pl.)	Kinder**n**
Frauen (f. pl.)	Fraue**n**

Refer to your textbook for a small group of nouns called **WEAK NOUNS** or **N-NOUNS** that add **-en** to every case, except in the nominative. While small in number, some of these words, like **Student, Name,** and **Präsident** are common.

When case is not indicated by the form of the noun itself, it is the definite or indefinite article that accompanies the noun that reflects the case, number, and gender of the noun.

- masculine singular articles → four case forms

	Definite	**Indefinite**
Nominative	der	ein
Accusative	den	einen
Dative	dem	einem
Genitive	des	eines

- feminine singular articles → two case forms

	Definite	**Indefinite**
Nominative & Accusative	die	eine
Dative & Genitive	der	einer

- neuter singular articles → three case forms

	Definite	**Indefinite**
Nominative & Accusative	das	ein
Dative	dem	einem
Genitive	des	eines

- plural of all articles → three case forms

	Definite	**Indefinite**
Nominative & Accusative	die	keine
Dative	den	keinen
Genitive	der	keiner

Below is a chart illustrating how nouns and their accompanying definite articles work hand-in-hand to indicate case.

- **DER** – indicates nominative case of singular masculine nouns, ex. **der Mann** *(the man)*
- **DIE** – indicates nominative case of singular feminine nouns, ex. **die Frau** *(the woman)*

- **DAS** – indicates nominative case of singular neuter nouns, ex. **das Kind** *(the child)*
- **DIE** – indicates the plural of all the cases of all genders, ex. **die Männer, die Frauen, die Kinder**

Notice that the singular form of the noun itself can change when made plural (**Mann,** sing. → **Männer,** pl.). Be sure to memorize the chart below, and as you learn new vocabulary, to note the nouns that change form in the plural.

	Singular			Plural
	Masculine	**Feminine**	**Neuter**	
Nominative	**der** Mann	**die** Frau	**das** Kind	**die** Kinder
Accusative	**den** Mann	**die** Frau	**das** Kind	**die** Kinder
Dative	**dem** Mann	**der** Frau	**dem** Kind	**den** Kinder**n**
Genitive	**des** Mann**es**	**der** Frau	**des** Kind**es**	**der** Kinder

To choose the appropriate case for nouns in a sentence, you need to go through a series of steps.

Here is an example.

The mother gives the child the apple.

1. **GENDER** – Identify the gender and number of each noun.

   the mother → die Mutter → feminine singular
   the child → das Kind → neuter singular
   the apple → der Apfel → masculine singular

2. **FUNCTION** – Determine the function of each noun.

   the mother → subject
   the child → indirect object
   the apple → direct object

3. **CASE** – Determine what case in German corresponds to the function identified in step 2.

   the mother → subject → nominative case
   the child → indirect object → dative case
   the apple → direct object → accusative case

4. **SELECTION** – Choose the proper form from the declension you have memorized.

   Die Mutter gibt **dem** Kind **den** Apfel.

Die	dem	den
feminine singular nominative	neuter singular dative	masculine singular accusative

Once the nouns are in their proper case, words in a sentence can be moved around without changing its meaning. Look at the many ways the English sentence above can be expressed in German.

> **Die** Mutter gibt **dem** Kind **den** Apfel.
> the mother gives to the child the apple
>
> **Den** Apfel gibt **die** Mutter **dem** Kind.
> **Dem** Kind gibt **die** Mutter **den** Apfel.

8.4 SUMMARY

- *who* or *what* is doing the action of the verb → subject → nominative case
- *who* or *what* is the direct recipient of the action of the verb → direct object → accusative case (a few verbs take the dative case).
- *who* or *what* is the indirect recipient of the action of the verb → indirect object → dative case
- *something* belongs to *someone* → possession → genitive case

Your textbook will explain in greater detail how to use the different case forms for the definite and indefinite articles. As you learn more German, you will discover other ways in which case affects the form of nouns (p. 9), pronouns (p. 38), and adjectives (p. 116).

STUDY TIPS
CASE

Flashcards

Using the chart on page 36, make cards illustrating each case by writing the German noun and accompanying article on one side; on the other side, indicate the gender, case, and number of the noun.

dem Kind	neuter, dative, singular
einer Frau	feminine, dative or genitive, singular
die Kinder	neuter, nominative or accusative, plural

While many case endings are similar, notice that the **-m** ending only occurs in the dative singular and that **-es** only occurs in the genitive singular for the masculine and neuter genders. Your textbook will go over the exceptions.

9 WHAT IS A PRONOUN?

A **PRONOUN** is a word used in place of one or more nouns (Nouns, p. 9). It may stand, therefore, for a person, place, thing, or idea.

> Karen likes to sing. She practices every day.
> noun pronoun

In the example above, the pronoun *she* refers to the proper noun *Karen*. A pronoun is almost always used to refer to someone, something, or an idea that has already been mentioned. The word that the pronoun replaces is called the **ANTECEDENT** of the pronoun. *Karen* is the antecedent of the pronoun *she*.

9.1 IN ENGLISH

There are different types of pronouns, each serving a different function and following different rules. The list below presents the most important types and refers you to the section where they are discussed.

PERSONAL PRONOUNS (p. 40) — These pronouns refer to different persons or things *(i.e., me, you, her, it)* and they change their form according to the function they have in a sentence.
The personal pronouns include:

SUBJECT PRONOUNS (p. 46) — These pronouns are used as the subject of a verb.

> *I* go.
> *They* read.
> *He* runs.

OBJECT PRONOUNS — These pronouns are used as:

- direct objects of a verb (p. 63)
  > Tina loves *him.*
  > Mark saw *them* at the theater.
- indirect objects of a verb (p. 65)
  > The boy wrote *me* the letter.
  > Petra gave *us* the book.
- objects of a preposition (p. 80)
  > Angela is going to the movies with *us.*
  > Don't step on *it;* walk around *it.*

REFLEXIVE PRONOUNS (p. 93) — These pronouns refer back to the subject of the sentence.

> I cut *myself.*
> She spoke about *herself.*

INTERROGATIVE PRONOUNS (p. 139) — These pronouns are used in questions.

> *Who* is that?
> *What* do you want?

POSSESSIVE PRONOUNS (p. 134) — These pronouns are used to show possession.

> Whose book is that? *Mine.*
> *Yours* is on the table.

RELATIVE PRONOUNS (p. 168) — These pronouns are used to introduce relative subordinate clauses.

> The man *who* came is very nice.
> Ingrid, *whom* you met, wants to study in Berlin.

9.2 IN GERMAN

Pronouns are identified in the same way as in English. The most important difference is that German pronouns have more forms than English pronouns since they must agree in gender, number, and case with the noun they replace (Gender, p. 21, Number, p. 16; Case p. 32).

You'll find a detailed discussion of German pronouns in the chapters referred to under In English above.

REVIEW ACTIVITY

Circle the pronouns in the sentences below. Draw an arrow from the pronoun to its antecedent(s).

a. Did Brooke phone? Yes, she called a few minutes ago.

b. Molly and Stan were out. They had a lot of errands to run.

c. If the paper is not next to the chair, look under it.

d. Sara injured herself on the playground.

e. Has Brad met Helga yet? Yes, Brad already knows her.

f. The Second World War ended in 1945. It lasted six long years.

10 WHAT IS A PERSONAL PRONOUN?

A **PERSONAL PRONOUN** is a word used to refer to a person, animal, thing or concept that has previously been mentioned.

Axel reads a book. *He* reads *it*.
He is a pronoun replacing a person, *Axel*.
It is a pronoun replacing a thing, *book*.

The books belong to Jade. *They* belong to *her*.
They is a personal pronoun replacing more than one thing, *books*.
Her is a personal pronoun replacing a person, *Jade*.

Freedom is precious. Many have died defending *it*.
It is a personal pronoun replacing a concept, *freedom*.

In English and in German personal pronouns are usually referred to by the **PERSON** to which they belong. The word "person" in this instance is a grammatical term that does not necessarily mean a human being; it can also refer to an animal, a thing or a concept. There are three persons: the 1st, 2nd and 3rd and each person has two forms, a singular form and a plural form, depending on whether it refers to one or more persons.

In both languages a different form of the personal pronoun is used depending on its function in a sentence; as subject, object or object of a preposition. These forms, called **CASE FORMS**, are discussed in separate chapters (Subject, p. 46; Objects, p. 68; Object of preposition, p. 80).

To introduce personal pronouns in this chapter we limit examples to personal pronouns used as subjects.

10.1 IN ENGLISH

Below are the forms of the subject personal pronouns. Sometimes, as in the case of the 3rd person singular, more than one pronoun *(he, she,* and *it)* belongs to the same person.

1ST PERSON

I → person speaking → **singular**
we → person speaking plus others → **plural**
Hans and I are free this evening. *We* are going out.

2ND PERSON

you → person or persons spoken to → **singular** or **plural**
Lukas, do *you* sing folk songs?
Johan, Kurt and Tina, do *you* sing folk songs?

3RD PERSON

he, she, it → person or object spoken about → **singular**
they → persons or objects spoken about → **plural**
Lukas cannot come along. *He* has to work.
Tina and Axel are free this evening. *They* are going out.

As you can see above, all the personal pronouns, except *you*, show whether one person or more than one is involved. For instance, the singular *I* is used by the person who is speaking to refer to himself or herself, and the plural *we* is used by the person speaking to refer to himself or herself plus others.

10.2 IN GERMAN

German personal pronouns are also identified as 1st, 2nd, and 3rd persons, each having a singular and a plural form. They are usually presented in the following order:

Singular			
1st person	*I*	ich	
2nd person	*you*	du	Familiar
		Sie	Formal
3rd person	*he*	er	Masculine
	she	sie	Feminine
	it	er	Masculine
		sie	Feminine
		es	Neuter
Plural			
1st person	we	wir	
2nd person	*you*	ihr	Familiar
		Sie	Formal
3rd person	*they*	sie	

To help you choose the correct "person", let us look at the English pronouns that have more than one equivalent in German: *you* and *it.*

10.3 "YOU"

IN ENGLISH

The same pronoun "you" is used to address one or more than one person.

> Ann, are *you* coming with me?
> Ann and Lukas, are *you* coming with me?

The same pronoun "you" is used to address anyone (person or animal), regardless of their rank.

> Do *you* have any questions, Mr. President?
> *You* are a good dog, Spot.

IN GERMAN

There are two sets of pronouns for *you*, the **FAMILIAR FORM** and the **FORMAL FORM.**

FAMILIAR "YOU" → DU OR IHR

The familiar forms of *you* are used to address members of one's family (notice that the word "familiar" is similar to the word "family"), persons you call by their first name, children, and pets.

- to address one person (2nd person singular) → **du**

 Jade, are you there?
 du

 Axel, are you there?
 du

- to address more than one person (2nd person plural) to whom you would say **du** individually → **ihr**

 Jade and Axel, are you there?
 ihr

FORMAL "YOU" → SIE

The formal form of *you* is used to address persons you do not know well enough to call by their first name or to whom you should show respect (Ms. Smith, Mr. Jones, Dr. Anderson, Professor Schneider). There is only one form, **Sie**, regardless of whether you are addressing one or more persons.

 Professor Schneider, are you there?
 Sie

 Professor Schneider and Mrs. Schneider, are you there?
 Sie

Note that the formal *you* form **Sie** is always capitalized. It should help you distinguish it from **sie** the German pronoun for *she* and for *they*.

If in doubt as to whether to use the familiar or formal form when addressing an adult, use the formal form. It shows respect for the person you are talking to, and the use of the familiar form might be considered rude.

10.4 "IT"

IN ENGLISH

Whenever you are speaking about one thing or idea, you use the personal pronoun *it*.

 Where is the pencil? *It* is on the table.
 Axel has an idea. *It* is very interesting.

When there is no reference to a specific noun, you use *it*.

 It is raining.

IN GERMAN

The personal pronoun used depends on the gender of the German noun *it* replaces, i.e., its antecedent. Thus *it* can be either masculine, feminine, or neuter (Chap 20).

To choose the correct form of *it*, you must identify two things:

- **ANTECEDENT** – Find the noun *it* replaces.
- **GENDER** – Determine the gender of the German word for the antecedent.

Here are some examples:

- masculine antecedent → **er**

    *Where is the suitcase? **It** is next to the chair.*

    ANTECEDENT: the suitcase
    GENDER: **Der Koffer** *(suitcase)* is masculine.

    Wo ist der Koffer? **Er** ist neben dem Stuhl.
    masculine

- feminine antecedent → **sie**

    *How was the trip ? **It** was nice.*

    ANTECEDENT: the trip
    GENDER: **Die Reise** *(trip)* is feminine.

    Wie war die Reise? **Sie** war sehr schön.
    feminine

- neuter antecedent → **es**

    *When does the plane leave? **It** leaves at 10 o'clock.*

    ANTECEDENT: the plane
    GENDER: **Das Flugzeug** *(plane)* is neuter.

    Wann fliegt das Flugzeug ab? **Es** fliegt um 10 Uhr ab.
    neuter

- no reference to a specific noun → **es**

    ***It** is raining.*
    Es regnet.
    neuter

STUDY TIPS
PERSONAL PRONOUNS

Flashcards

Make a flashcard for each personal pronoun, with a separate card for the four forms of you: singular familiar; singular formal; plural familiar; plural formal.

As you learn nouns, write the associated pronoun alongside it. This creates and reinforces a visual connection to grammatical gender in articles and pronouns.

die Katze, die Katzen (sie)

WHAT IS A SUBJECT? 11

In a sentence the person or thing that performs the action of the verb is called the **SUBJECT.**

11.1 IN ENGLISH

To find the subject of a sentence, always look for the verb first; then ask *who?* or *what?* before the verb (Verb, p. 29). The answer will be the subject.

Axel studies German.
VERB: studies
Who studies German? ANSWER: Axel.
Axel is the subject.
The subject is singular (Number, p. 16). It refers to one person.

Did the packages come yesterday?
VERB: come
What came yesterday? ANSWER: packages.
Packages is the subject.
The subject is plural. It refers to more than one thing.

If a sentence has more than one main verb, you have to find the subject of each verb.

The boys were cooking while Jade set the table.
Boys is the subject of *were.*
Note that the subject is plural.
Jade is the subject of *set.*
Note that the subject is singular.

11.2 IN GERMAN

In German it is particularly important that you recognize the subject of a sentence so that you can put it in the proper case (Case, p. 32). The subject of a German sentence is in the nominative case. Unlike in English, in German you may find the subject after the verb rather than in front of it. Pay attention to the words on either side of the verb to help locate the subject.

***The child** plays alone.*
Who plays? ANSWER: the child
Child **(das Kind)** is the subject, therefore **das Kind** is in the nominative case.
Das kind spielt allein.

*On Tuesdays **the children** play soccer.*
Who plays? ANSWER: *the children*
Children **(die Kinder)** is the subject, therefore **die Kinder** is in the nominative case.
Dienstags spielen **die Kinder** Fußball.
on Tuesdays play the children soccer

CAREFUL – In English and in German it is important to find the subject of each verb so that you can choose the form of the verb that goes with each subject.

12 WHAT IS A SUBJECT PRONOUN?

Pronouns used as subjects are called **SUBJECT PRONOUNS** (Pronouns, p. 38; Subject, p. 45).

> *They* ran, but *I* walked.
>> Who ran? ANSWER: They.
>> *They* is the subject of the verb *ran*.
>> Who walked? ANSWER: I.
>> *I* is the subject of the verb *walked*.

12.1 IN ENGLISH

Below is a list of English subject pronouns, also referred to as **NOMINATIVE PRONOUNS.** For an explanation of the various "persons" see p 40.

Singular	
1st person	I
2nd person	you
3rd person	he, she, it
Plural	
1st person	we
2nd person	you
3rd person	they

The above personal pronouns are used as subjects of a verb or as predicate nominatives (Predicates, p. 48). English uses another set of pronouns when the pronoun is an object of a verb (Object pronouns, p. 68) or of a preposition (Object of preposition pronouns, p. 80).

12.2 IN GERMAN

The **NOMINATIVE CASE** of the pronoun is used for the subject of the verb (Verb, p. 29; Case, p. 32). To help you select the proper German subject pronoun see below.

	English	German	
	Nominative		
Singular			
1st person	*I*	ich	
2nd person	*you*	du	Familiar
		Sie	Formal
3rd person	*he*	er	Masculine
	she	sie	Feminine
	it	er	Masculine
		sie	Feminine
		es	Neuter
Plural			
1st person	we	wir	
2nd person	*you*	ihr	Familiar
		Sie	Formal
3rd person	*they*	sie	

REVIEW ACTIVITY

Find the subjects in the sentences below.

I. Next to Q, write the question you need to ask to find the subject of the entence above.
II. Next to A, write the answer to the question you just asked.
III. Circle if the subject is singular **(S)** or plural **(P).**

a. I go to college in the fall.
Q: ______________________________
A: ______________________________ S P

b. My bother and sister are still in high school.
Q: ______________________________
A: ______________________________ S P

c. During the school year, they don't work.
Q: ______________________________
A: ______________________________ S P

d. Unlike my siblings, I have to work all year long.
Q: ______________________________
A: ______________________________ S P

13 WHAT IS A PREDICATE NOUN?

A **PREDICATE NOUN** is a noun connected to the subject by a linking verb. A **LINKING VERB** is a verb that acts as an equal sign linking interchangeable elements (Nouns, p. 9; Verb, p. 29).

Johan is my friend. [Johan = friend]
subject | predicate noun
linking verb

13.1 IN ENGLISH

The most common linking verbs are *to be* and *to become*. The noun that follows the linking verb is not an object because it does not receive the action of the verb (Objects, p. 63), instead, it is a predicate noun because it is interchangeable with the subject.

Ingrid is a good *student*.
linking verb predicate noun
LINKING VERB: is (form of *to be*)
SUBJECT: Ingrid
PREDICATE NOUN: student (Ingrid = student)

Axel became a *teacher*.
linking verb predicate noun
LINKING VERB: became (form of *to become*)
SUBJECT: Axel
PREDICATE NOUN: teacher (Axel = teacher)

13.2 IN GERMAN

The most common linking verbs are **sein** *(to be)*, **werden** *(to become)* and **bleiben** *(to remain)*. As in English, the noun following a linking verb is a predicate noun, not an object. Predicate nouns are in the nominative case, the same case as the subject (Case, p. 32).

Ingrid ist eine gute **Studentin**.
nom. case | linking verb | nom. case
LINKING VERB: **ist** (form of **sein** *to be*)
SUBJECT = PREDICATE NOUN: **Ingrid = Studentin** (*student*)
Both **Ingrid** and **Studentin** are in the nominative case.
Ingrid is a good ***student.***

Axel wurde **Lehrer**.
nom. case | linking verb | nom. case
LINKING VERB: **wurde** (form of **werden** to *become*)
SUBJECT = PREDICATE NOUN: **Axel = Lehrer** (*teacher*)
Both **Axel** and **Lehrer** are in the nominative case.
Axel became a ***teacher.***

CAREFUL – It is important that you distinguish predicate nouns from objects so that you can put them in the appropriate case, i. e., the nominative case.

STUDY TIPS
PREDICATE NOUNS

Flashcards

On the English side of your cards for the verbs **sein, werden,** and **scheinen** indicate "linking verb, predicate noun takes nominative case (N)", with an example.

Herr Meier ist der Lehrer.
N N

REVIEW ACTIVITY

Circle the predicate noun in the following sentences. Draw an arrow from the predicate noun to the subject with which it is linked.

a. The letter was really good news.

b. Carol became a doctor.

c. They are tourists.

d. Dan became an accomplished musician.

e. The swimming pool is our favorite place in the summer.

f. The current situation remains a big challenge for us.

14 WHAT IS A VERB CONJUGATION?

A **VERB CONJUGATION** is a list of the six possible forms of a verb for a particular tense (Tense, p. 59). For each tense, there is one verb form for each of the six persons used as the subject of the verb (Subject pronouns, p. 46).

Different tenses have different verb forms, but the principle of conjugation remains the same. In this chapter our examples are in the present tense (Present, p. 61).

Singular

1st person	I am
2nd person	you are
3rd person	he, she, it is

Plural

1st person	we are
2nd person	you are
3rd person	they are

14.1 IN ENGLISH

The verb *to be* conjugated above is the English verb that changes the most; it has three forms: *am*, *are*, and *is*. In conversation the initial vowel is often replaced by an apostrophe: *I'm*, *you're*, *he's*. Other English verbs only have two forms. Let us look at the verb *to sing*.

Singular

1st person	I sing
2nd person	you sing
3rd person	he sing**s** she sing**s** it sing**s**

Plural

1st person	we sing
2nd person	you sing
3rd person	they sing

Because English verbs change so little, it isn't necessary to learn "to conjugate a verb;" that is, to list all its possible forms. For most verbs, it is much simpler to say that the verb adds an "(e)-s" in the 3rd person singular.

14.2 IN GERMAN

Unlike English, German verb forms change from one person to another so that when you learn a new verb you must also learn how to conjugate it. The conjugation of most verbs follows a predictable pattern so that once you learn the pattern for one German verb you will be able to apply that pattern to other German verbs.

CATEGORIES OF GERMAN VERBS

A German verb is composed of two parts, a stem and an ending.

- **THE STEM** – the part of the verb left after dropping the final **-en** from the infinitive (or with a few verbs like **tun** *to do* and **ändern** *to change* by dropping the final **-n**).
- **THE ENDING** – the part of the verb that is added at the end of the stem and that corresponds to the grammatical person.

Infinitive	Stem	Ending present tense	
sing**en**	sing-	ich sing**e**	(1st pers. sing.)
mach**en**	mach-	du mach**st**	(2nd pers. sing.)
komm**en**	komm-	sie komm**t**	(3rd pers. sing.)

Listed below is the terminology used to categorize German verbs according to the changes in the stem. You will notice that some verbs belong to more than one category.

WEAK VERBS (sometimes called **REGULAR VERBS**) — verbs that keep the same stem throughout the different tenses. For example, **wohn**en, **wohn**te, ge**wohn**t (*live, lived, lived*).

STRONG VERBS (sometimes called **IRREGULAR VERBS**) — verbs whose stem vowel changes to indicate different tenses. For example, **sing**en, **sang**, ge**sung**en (*sing, sang, sung*). Note that strong verbs are not exactly irregular—they belong to a limited number of verb groups with similar patterns of vowel changes.

STEM-CHANGING VERBS – verbs whose stem vowel changes in the 2nd and 3rd person singular of the present tense. For example, **lesen** *(to read)*, **du liest, er liest** *(you read, he reads)*. The stem change can also be the addition of an umlaut over the vowel. For examples, **fahren** *(to travel)*, **du fährst, er fährst** *(you travel, he travels)*.

Some verbs belong to the two above categories: for instance, **geben** *(to give)* is a stem-changing verb since the stem vowel changes from **-e-** to **-i-** in the 2nd and 3rd person singular in the present tense; it is also a strong verb since the stem vowel changes from **-e-** to **a-** depending on the tense.

MIXED VERBS — verbs that have elements of both weak and strong verbs. Many common verbs are mixed verbs: **bringen** *(to bring)*, **kennen** *(to know)*, **denken** *(to think)*.

When you learn a new verb, memorize in which category it belongs so that you can conjugate it correctly.

Note: The English verb system also includes weak, strong, and mixed verbs which can be recognized by the similar conjugation patterns (weak: *play-played*, strong: *sing-sang*, mixed: *bring, brought*). While not every pair of verbs in both languages will always share the same pattern, they usually do and it helps to recognize the similarities.

14.2

HOW TO CONJUGATE A VERB

Here are the steps to conjugate the regular verb **machen** *(to make)* in the present tense.

1. Find the verb stem by removing the infinitive ending.

   INFINITIVE: **machen** → STEM: **mach-**

2. Add the ending that agrees with the subject. Weak and strong verbs add the same endings in the present tense.

Singular

1st person	ich mach**e**	*I make*
2nd person familiar	du mach**st**	*you make*
3rd person	er mach**t**	*he, it makes*
	sie mach**t**	*she, it makes*
	es mach**t**	*it makes*

Plural

1st person	wir mach**en**	*we make*
2nd person familiar	ihr mach**t**	*you make*
3rd person	sie mach**en**	*they make*
2nd person formal (sing. & pl.)	Sie mach**en**	*you make*

As strong verbs are introduced in your textbook, either their entire conjugation or their principal parts will be given so that you will know how to conjugate them (Principal parts, p. 82). Be sure to memorize these forms, because many common verbs are irregular (**sein**, *to be;* **gehen**, *to go;* **werden,** *to become*, for example).

CHOOSING THE CORRECT "PERSON"

(Personal pronouns, p. 40)

In your textbook, the 2nd person formal forms will either be listed after the 2nd person familiar plural forms or after the 3rd person plural form, as they are in the conjugation of the verb **singen** (*to sing*) below.

Singular

1st person	ich singe	*I sing*
2nd person familiar	du singst	*you sing*
3rd person	er singt	*he, it sings*
	sie singt	*she, it sings*
	es singt	*it sings*

Plural

1st person	wir singen	*we sing*
2nd person familiar	ihr singt	*you sing*
3rd person	sie singen	*they sing*
2nd person formal (sing. & pl.)	Sie singen	*you sing*

To choose the proper verb form, it is important to identify the person and the number of the subject.

1ST PERSON SINGULAR – The subject is always **ich** *(I)*. Notice that **ich** is not capitalized unless it is the first word of a sentence.

Ich singe leise.
I sing softly.

Leise singe **ich**.
*Softly **I** sing.*

2ND PERSON SINGULAR FAMILIAR – The subject is always **du** (*you*).

Katrin, **du** singst gut.
*Katrin, **you** sing well.*

3RD PERSON SINGULAR – The subject can be expressed in one of three ways:

- the 3rd person singular masculine pronoun **er** *(he* or *it)*, the feminine pronoun **sie** *(she* or *it)*, and the neuter pronoun **es** *(it)*

  Er singt schön.
  ***He** sings beautifully.*

  Sie singt schön.
  ***She** sings beautifully.*

  Es singt schön.
  ***It** sings beautifully.*

- a proper noun

  Anna singt gut.
  ***Anna** sings well.*

  Der Fischer Chor singt gut.
  ***The Fischer choir** sings well.*

  Since the proper noun could be replaced by the pronoun *he, she* or *it* (**er, sie**, or **es**), you must use the 3rd person singular form of the verb.

- a singular common noun

  Der Vogel singt.
  ***The bird** sings.*

  Die Geige singt.
  ***The violin** sings.*

Das Kind singt.
The child sings.
Since the common noun could be replaced by the pronoun *he, she* or *it* (**er, sie**, or **es**), you must use the 3rd person singular form of the verb.

1ST PERSON PLURAL – The subject can be expressed in one of two ways:

- the 1st person plural pronoun **wir** *(we)*

Wir singen gut.
We sing well.

- a multiple subject in which the speaker is included

Axel, Lukas, Ingrid und ich singen gut.
Axel, Lukas, Ingrid and I sing well.
Since the subject could be replaced by the pronoun *we* (**wir**), you must use the 1st person plural form of the verb.

2ND PERSON PLURAL FAMILIAR – The subject is always **ihr** *(you).*

Ingrid und Lukas, singt **ihr** auch?
*Ingrid and Lukas, do **you** sing too?*
Since the subjects *Ingrid* and *Lukas* (whom you would address with the 2nd person familiar individually), could be replaced by the pronoun *you* (**ihr**), you must use the 2nd person plural familiar form of the verb.

2ND PERSON FORMAL (SINGULAR AND PLURAL) – The subject is always **Sie** *(you).* Notice that **Sie** is always capitalized regardless of its position in a sentence.

Frau Meier, wollen **Sie** heute nicht singen?
*Mrs. Meier, do **you** not want to sing today?*

Herr und Frau Meier, singen **Sie** gern zusammen?
*Mr. and Mrs. Meier, do **you** like to sing together?*
Since the subjects *Mr.* and *Mrs. Meier* (whom you would address with the 2nd person formal individually or together) could be replaced by the pronoun *you* (**Sie**), you must use the 2nd person formal form of the verb.

3RD PERSON PLURAL – The subject can be expressed in one of three ways:

- the 3rd person plural pronoun **sie** *(they)*

Sie singen im Chor.
They sing in the choir.

- a plural noun

Die Kinder singen im Chor.
The children sing in the choir.
The plural noun could be replaced by the 3rd person plural pronoun *they* (**sie**), you must use the 3rd person plural form of the verb.

- two or more proper or common nouns

Lukas und Ingrid singen ein Duett.
Lukas and Ingrid sing a duet.

Die Gläser und Teller sind auf dem Tisch.
The glasses and plates are on the table.

The nouns could be replaced by the 3rd person plural pronoun *they* (**sie**), you must use the 3rd person plural form of the verb.

STUDY TIPS
VERB CONJUGATIONS

Pattern

① Start by looking for a pattern within the conjugation of the verb itself. For example, let's find a pattern in the conjugation of **wohnen**.

ich wohne	wir wohnen
du wohnst	ihr wohnt
er/sie/es wohnt	sie wohnen/Sie Wohnen

What pattern do you see?

- all the forms start with the same stem: **wohn-** and **mach-**
- **ich** forms have an **-e** ending
- **du** forms have an **-st** ending
- **er/sie/es** and **ihr** have a **-t** ending
- **wir, sie** (pl.) and **Sie** have an **-en** ending

If you learn best with mnemonics, think of the regular conjugation pattern as the verb stem + **-e, -st, 10, 10** throughout the list; that is, **-e, -st, -t, -en, -t, -en** for **ich, du, er/sie/es, wir, ihr,** and **Sie/sie**. Your teacher may also share this mnemonic in the form of "icky dust 10 10" **(ich -e, du -st, -t, -en, -t, -en).**

② Whenever you learn a new verb, look for similarities with another verb. The pattern can be related to the consonant ending the stem. For example, let's look at **fin<u>d</u>en** *(to find)*, **arbei<u>t</u>en** *(to work)* and **öff<u>n</u>en** *(to open)*.

ich finde	wir finden	ich arbeite	wir arbeiten	ich öffne	wir öffnen
du find**est**	ihr find**et**	du arbeit**est**	ihr arbeit**et**	du öffn**est**	ihr öffn**et**
er find**et**	sie/Sie finden	er arbeit**et**	sie/Sie arbeiten	er öffn**et**	sie/Sie öffnen

What similarities and differences with regular verbs (see under 1 above) do you see?

- the endings of the verb forms are the same, except for **du, er/sie/es** and **ihr** that insert an **-e** before the ending

The pattern can be related to the vowel of the stem. For example, let's look at three stem-changing verbs **s<u>e</u>hen** *(to see)*, **schl<u>a</u>fen** *(to sleep)* and **g<u>e</u>ben** *(to give)*.

ich sehe	wir sehen	ich schlafe	wir schlafen	ich gebe	wir geben
du s**ie**hst	ihr seht	du schl**ä**fst	ihr schlaft	du g**i**bst	ihr gebt
er s**ie**ht	sie/Sie sehen	er schl**ä**ft	sie/Sie schlafen	er g**i**bt	sie/Sie geben

What similarities and differences with regular verbs (see under 1 above) do you see?

- the endings of all the verb forms are the same
- the stem vowel changes only in the **du** and **er/sie/es** forms
- vowels change in the same way in the **du** and **er/sie/es** forms

(3) In the conjugation of most regular and irregular German verbs, there are four forms that look like the infinitive of the verb and end in **-en** or **-n:** the 1st and 3rd persons plural and the 2nd person formal, singular and plural (Verbs, p. 29).

(4) As new verb conjugations are introduced, more and more similarities and patterns will become evident. Take the time to look for them.

Flashcards

Create a card for each verb to memorize its meaning and conjugation pattern. On the German side, write the infinitive form and the following information as appropriate:

(1) If it is a stem-changing verb, indicate its type **(a → ä; e → i; e → ie)** in parentheses.

fahren (a → ä)	*to drive*
geben (e → i)	*to give*
lesen (e → ie)	*to read*

(2) If the verb requires a spelling change in the **du** or **er/sie/es** endings owing to particular consonant combinations, write the form in parentheses and underline the spelling change.

reden (er red<u>e</u>t)	*to talk*
arbeiten (er arbeit<u>e</u>t)	*to work*
tanzen (du tan<u>z</u>t)	*to dance*

Practice

1. Learn the different forms of a verb by writing them down (always using the subject pronoun). Repeat until you can write the correct forms without referring to your textbook.
2. Practice using the various forms out of order, so that if you are asked a question you can respond without going through the entire pattern.
3. Be sure to do the exercises that follow the introduction of a new conjugation. When you've finished, refer to your textbook or answer key to make corrections. Mark the mistakes and corrections with a colored pen so that they stand out and you can concentrate on them when you review.
4. Write your own sentences using the different forms of the verb.

See also Study Tips, p. 84.

REVIEW ACTIVITY

I. Draw a box around the stem of the German verbs in the infinitive form.

a. denken
b. rennen
c. arbeiten
d. wandern
e. reisen
f. tun
g. vertreten
h. mitnehmen

II. Write the stem and conjugate the verbs.

a. gehen (to go). Stem:____________________

ich____________________

du____________________

er, sie, es____________________

wir____________________

ihr____________________

sie____________________

b. laufen (to run). Stem: ____________________

ich____________________

du____________________

er, sie, es____________________

wir____________________

ihr____________________

sie____________________

WHAT IS MEANT BY TENSE? 15

The **TENSE** of a verb indicates when the action of the verb takes place: at the present time, in the past, or in the future.

I am saying	Present
I said	Past
I will say	Future

As you can see in the above examples, just by putting the verb in a different tense, and without giving any additional information (such as "I am saying it *now*", "I said it *yesterday*", "I will say it *tomorrow*"), you can indicate when the action of the verb takes place.

Tenses may be classified according to the way they are formed. A **SIMPLE TENSE** consists of only one verb form, "I *said*", while a **COMPOUND TENSE** consists of one or more auxiliaries plus the main verb, "I *am saying, I have said*" (Auxiliary verbs, p. 88).

In this section we will only consider tenses of the indicative mood (Mood, p 178).

15.1 IN ENGLISH

Listed below are the main tenses of the indicative mood whose equivalents you will encounter in German.

Present

I say	Present
I am saying	Present progressive
I do say	Present emphatic

Past

I said	Simple past
I did say	Past emphatic
I have said	Present perfect
I was saying	Past progressive
I had said	Past perfect

Future

I will say	Future
I will have said	Future perect

As you can see, there are only two simple tenses: present and simple past. All the other tenses are compound tenses.

15.2 IN GERMAN

Listed below are the main tenses of the indicative mood that you will encounter in German.

Present		
ich sage	*I say, I do say* *I am saying*	Present
Past		
ich sagte	*I said, I did say* *I was saying*	Simple past/ Past progressive
ich habe gesagt	*I have said*	Present perfect
ich hatte gesagt	*I had said*	Past perfect
Future		
ich werde sagen	*I will say*	Future
ich werde gesagt haben	*I will have said*	Future perfect

As you can see, there are fewer present tense forms in German than in English; for example, there are no progressive forms.

This handbook discusses the various tenses and their usage in separate chapters: Present, p. 61; Future, p. 99; Past, p. 102; Past perfect, p. 112; Future perfect p. 114. Verb tenses can be grouped according to the mood in which they are used.

CAREFUL – Do not assume that tenses with the same name are used the same way in English and in German.

WHAT IS THE PRESENT TENSE? 16

The **PRESENT TENSE** indicates that the action of the verb is happening at the present time. It can be at the moment the speaker is speaking, a habitual action, or a general truth.

> I *see* you.
> He *laughs* when he *is* nervous.
> The sun *rises* every day.

16.1 IN ENGLISH

There are three verb forms that indicate the present tense. Each form has a slightly different meaning:

Anja *works* in the library.	Present
Anja *is working* in the library.	Present progressive
Anja *does work* in the library.	Present emphatic

Depending on the way a question is worded, you will automatically choose one of the three above forms.

> Where does Anja work? She *works* in the library.
> Where is Anja now? She *is working* in the library.
> Does Anja work in the library? Yes, she *does* [*work* in the library].

16.2 IN GERMAN

Unlike English, there is only one verb form to indicate the present tense. The German present tense is used to express the meaning of the English present, present progressive, and present emphatic tenses. The present tense in German is a simple tense formed by adding the present endings to the stem of the verb (Conjugation, p. 50).

> Anja *works* in the library.
> **arbeitet**
>
> Anja *is working* in the library.
> **arbeitet**
>
> Anja *does work* in the library.
> **arbeitet**

CAREFUL– Remember that in the present tense in German there is no need for auxiliary verbs such as *is, do, does;* do not try to include them.

REVIEW ACTIVITY

Circle the words that correspond to the German present tense.

a. So John and Vera really do play tennis.
b. Yes, John plays often.
c. In fact, Vera is playing right now too.
d. Our friends are playing with them.
e. Do you play too?

WHAT IS AN OBJECT? 17

An **OBJECT** is a noun or pronoun that receives the action of the verb or is associated with a preposition.

> Axel *writes* a letter.
> (*writes*: verb; *letter*: direct object)

> Axel *writes* his mother a letter.
> (*writes*: verb; *mother*: indirect object)

> The boy left *with* his father.
> (*with*: preposition; *father*: object of a preposition)

In this chapter we will study the direct object and the indirect object (the object of a preposition is covered in Chapter 19). Although we have limited the examples in this section to noun objects, the same questions can be used to establish the function of pronoun objects.

17.1 DIRECT OBJECT (ALSO SEE DIRECT AND INDIRECT OBJECT PRONOUNS, P. 68)

IN ENGLISH

A direct object is a noun or pronoun that receives the action of the verb directly, without a preposition between the verb and the noun or pronoun. It answers the question *whom?* or *what?* asked after the verb.

> Axel sees *Ingrid.*
> Axel sees *whom?* Ingrid.
> *Ingrid* is the direct object.

> Axel writes *a letter*.
> Axel writes *what?* A letter.
> *A letter* is the direct object.

There are two types of verbs: transitive and intransitive.

- **TRANSITIVE VERB** – a verb that takes a direct object. It is indicated by the abbreviation *v.t.* (verb transitive) or *trans.* in dictionaries.

  > The boy *threw* the ball.
  > (*threw*: transitive; *ball*: noun = direct object)

  > She *lost* her job.
  > (*lost*: transitive; *job*: noun = direct object)

- **INTRANSITIVE VERB** – a verb that cannot take a direct object. It is indicated by the abbreviation *v.i.* (verb intransitive) or *intrans.* in dictionaries.

Ingrid *arrives* today.
intransitive adverb

Franz *is sleeping.*
intransitive

Many verbs can be used both transitively, that is, with a direct object, and intransitively, without a direct object.

The students *speak* German.
transitive noun = direct object

Actions *speak* louder than words.
intransitive adverbial phrase

CAREFUL — Some verbs that are transitive in English are intransitive in German, while other verbs that are intransitive in English are transitive in German.

IN GERMAN

As in English, a direct object is a noun or pronoun that receives the action of the verb directly. It answers the question **wen?** *(whom?)* or **was?** *(what?)* asked after the verb. Direct objects are expressed by the accusative case in German (Case, p. 32).

Niko liest **das Buch.**
Niko reads *what?* The book.
Das Buch is the direct object → accusative case
Niko reads ***the book.***

A few verbs take dative case direct objects in German instead of accusative case direct objects. These are referred to as **DATIVE VERBS**. Here are two examples.

- **danken** *(to thank)*

Sie danken **dem Polizisten.**
They thank *whom?* The police officer **(dem Polizisten)**.
Dem Polizisten is the direct object, but in the dative case.
They thank ***the police officer.***

- **helfen** *(to help)*

Wir helfen **dir**.
We are helping *whom*? You **(dir)**.
Dir is the direct object, but in the dative case.
We are helping ***you.***

Other common dative verbs include **folgen** *(follow)*, **gefallen** *(like)*, **antworten** *(answer)*, and **glauben** *(believe)*.

Verbs whose direct objects are expressed in the dative do not also have indirect objects (see below). Your German textbook will indicate the verbs that take direct objects in the dative case, and you will need to memorize them.

CAREFUL – An English verb that requires a preposition before its object may have an equivalent German verb that requires a direct object in the accusative.

She is looking for ***her coat.***
She is looking *for what? Her coat* is the object of the preposition *for*.

Sie sucht **ihren Mantel**.
suchen *(to look for)* takes a direct object → **ihren mantel** → accusative case

17.2 INDIRECT OBJECT (ALSO SEE DIRECT AND INDIRECT OBJECT PRONOUNS, P. 68)

IN ENGLISH

An indirect object is a noun or pronoun that receives the action of the verb indirectly. It answers the question *to* or *for whom?* or *to* or *for what?* asked after the verb.

Axel wrote *his brother* a letter.
He wrote a letter *to whom?* His brother.
His brother is the indirect object.

Axel did *his brother* a favor.
He did a favor *for whom?* His brother.
His brother is the indirect object.

Sometimes the word *to* is included in the English sentence.

Axel spoke *to Lukas* and *Ingrid.*
Axel spoke *to whom?* To Lukas and Ingrid.
Lukas and *Ingrid* are two indirect objects.

IN GERMAN

As in English, an indirect object is a noun or pronoun that receives the action of the verb indirectly. It answers the question **wem?** *(to* or *for whom?)* or **was?** *(to* or *for what?)* asked after the verb. Indirect objects are expressed by the dative case in German.

Niko schreibt **seinem Bruder**.
Niko writes a letter *to whom?* His brother.
Seinem Bruder is the indirect object → dative case

Niko writes (to) ***his brother.***

Ingrid tat **mir** einen Gefallen.
Ingrid did a favor *for whom?* Me.
Mir is the indirect object → dative case

Ingrid did ***me*** *a favor.*

Note that in German there is no need for the prepositions "to" or "for", the dative case indicates that it is an indirect object.

17.3 SENTENCES WITH A DIRECT AND INDIRECT OBJECT

A sentence may contain both a direct object and an indirect object, either as nouns or pronouns.

IN ENGLISH

When a sentence has both a direct and an indirect object, two word orders are possible, one without "to" preceding the indirect object and one with the preposition "to".

- If the indirect object is not preceded by "to", the word order is as follows: subject (S) + verb (V) + indirect object (IO) + direct object (DO).

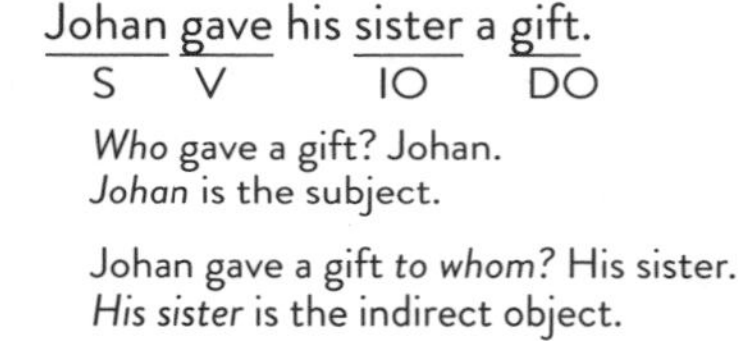

Johan gave his sister a gift.
S V IO DO

Who gave a gift? Johan.
Johan is the subject.

Johan gave a gift *to whom?* His sister.
His sister is the indirect object.

Johan gave *what?* A gift.
A gift is the direct object.

- If the indirect object is preceded by "to", the word order is as follows: subject + verb + direct object + *to* + indirect object.

Johan gave a gift to his sister.
S V DO to IO

Both forms are used in English. However, since there is no "to" preceding the indirect object *(sister),* in the first version, it is more difficult to identify its function than in the second structure.

IN GERMAN

As in English, a sentence can have both a direct and an indirect object. The order of the objects in the German sentence depends on whether they are nouns or pronouns and on their function. For example:

- noun objects → indirect object + direct object
- pronoun objects → direct object + indirect object
- pronoun and noun objects → pronoun + noun

While these patterns are helpful and necessary to memorize, the order of the objects can also depend on a particular word you want to emphasize. Consult your textbook for details.

REVIEW ACTIVITY

Find the objects in the sentences below:

I. Next to Q, write the question you need to ask to find the object.
II. Next to A, write the answer to the question you just asked.
III. Circle the kind of object it is: direct object **(DO),** indirect object **(IO)** or object of a preposition **(OP).**

a. The computer lost my homework.

Q: ______________________ DO IO OP

A: ______________________

b. She sent her friend a postcard.

Q: ______________________ DO IO OP

A: ______________________

Q: ______________________ DO IO OP

A: ______________________

c. My parents bought my brother those books.

Q: ______________________ DO IO OP

A: ______________________

Q: ______________________ DO IO OP

A: ______________________

18 WHAT ARE DIRECT AND INDIRECT OBJECT PRONOUNS?

An **OBJECT PRONOUN** is a pronoun used as an direct or indirect object (Pronouns, p. 38; Objects, p. 62).

> Axel saw *us*.
> > Axel saw *whom?* Us.
> > Pronoun *us* → direct object of *saw*
>
> My parents wrote *me* a letter.
> > My parents wrote a letter *to whom?* Me.
> > Pronoun *me* → indirect object of *wrote*

The various functions of object pronouns are established the same way as the function of object nouns.

18.1 IN ENGLISH

Most pronouns used as direct and indirect objects in English are different in form from the ones used as subjects (Subject, p. 46). In other words, this is the only English part of speech that reflects case by changing form according to its function: when the pronoun is a subject, it is in the **NOMINATIVE** form and when it is a direct or indirect object it is in the **OBJECTIVE** form.

	Subject nominative	**Object objective**
Singular		
1st person	I	me
2nd person	you	you
3rd person	he	him
	she	her
	it	it
Plural		
1st person	we	us
2nd person	you	you
3rd person	they	them

Here are a few examples of the usage of nominative and objective pronouns.

> He and I work for the newspaper.
> subjects: 3rd pers. sing. + 1st pers. sing.
> nominative case
>
> The politician invited him and me to lunch.
> direct objects: 3rd pers. sing. + 1st pers. sing.
> objective case
>
> They took their car to the garage.
> subject: 3rd pers. pl.
> nominative case

I lent *them* my car.
indirect object: 3rd pers. pl.
objective case

18.2 IN GERMAN

Unlike English, which has only one case for pronouns, objects, German uses two cases, the accusative and the dative. Look at the chart below.

	English objective	German accusative	German dative	
Singular				
1st person	me	mich	mir	
2nd person	you	dich	dir	Familiar
		Sie	Ihnen	Formal
3rd person	him	ihn	ihm	Masculine
	her	sie	ihr	Feminine
	it	es	ihm	Neuter
Plural				
1st person	us	uns	uns	
2nd person	you	euch	euch	Familiar
		Sie	Ihnen	Formal
3rd person	them	sie	ihnen	

Two English object pronouns have more than one equivalent in German: *you* and *it*. To help you choose the correct German object pronoun, let us look at the two English object pronouns.

FAMILIAR "YOU" AS OBJECT PRONOUN (Personal pronouns, p. 41)

The familiar forms of *you* can be singular or plural, depending on whether the *you* addressed is one or more persons, each form having an accusative and dative form.

- **SINGULAR** – You are speaking to one person → **dich** (acc.); **dir** (dat.)

  *We see **you**, Anna.*
  Wir sehen **dich**, Anna.
  sehen *(to see)* takes an accusative object

  *We are helping **you**, Anna.*
  Wir helfen **dir**, Anna.
  helfen *(to help)* takes a dative object

- **PLURAL** – You are speaking to more than one person → **euch** (acc. and dat.)

  *We see **you**, Effi and Franz.*
  Wir sehen **euch**, Effi und Franz.
  sehen *(to see)* takes an accusative object

  *We are helping **you**, Effi and Franz.*
  Wir helfen **euch,** Effi und Franz.
  helfen *(to help)* takes a dative object

FORMAL "YOU" AS OBJECT PRONOUN

The formal form of *you* has two forms, the accusative and the dative; the same form is used for the singular and the plural.

- **ACCUSATIVE** – You are speaking to one or more persons → **Sie** (acc. sing. and pl.)

  *We will see **you** tomorrow, Mrs. Erb.*
  Wir sehen **Sie** morgen, Frau Erb.
  sehen *(to see)* takes an accusative object

- **DATIVE** – You are speaking to one or more persons → **Ihnen** (dat. sing. and pl.)

  *We are glad to help **you**, Dr. Fried.*
  Wir helfen **Ihnen** gern, Dr. Fried.
  helfen *(to help)* takes a dative object

"IT" AS OBJECT PRONOUN (Personal pronouns, p. 42)

German has six different object pronouns equivalent to *it*, depending on the gender of the antecedent and the case of the pronoun (accusative or dative).

To choose the correct form, follow these steps:

1. ANTECEDENT: Find the noun *it* replaces.
2. GENDER: Determine the gender of the antecedent.
3. FUNCTION: Determine the function of *it* in the sentence: subject, direct object, indirect object, or object of a preposition.
4. CASE: Choose the case that corresponds to the function.
5. SELECTION: Select the form, depending on steps 2 and 4.

Let us look at some examples.

- **MASCULINE ANTECEDENT** → **ihn** (accusative) or **ihm** (dative)

  *Did you see the film? Yes, I saw **it**.*
  ANTECEDENT: the film
  GENDER: **der Film** *(the film)* → masculine
  FUNCTION: direct object of *see* **(sehen)**
  CASE: accusative
  SELECTION: masculine accusative → **ihn**

  Hast du den Film gesehen? Ja, ich habe **ihn** gesehen.

- **FEMININE ANTECEDENT** → **sie** (acc.) or **ihr** (dat.)

  *Are you reading the newspaper? Yes, I am reading **it.***
  ANTECEDENT: the newspaper
  GENDER: **die Zeitung** *(the newspaper)* → feminine
  FUNCTION: direct object of *read* **(lesen)**
  CASE: accusative
  SELECTION: feminine accusative → **sie**

  Lesen Sie die Zeitung? Ja, ich lese **sie**.

- **NEUTER ANTECEDENT** → **es** (acc.) or **ihm** (dat.)

  *Do you understand the book? Yes, I understand **it.***
  ANTECEDENT: the book
  GENDER: **das Buch** *(the book)* → neuter
  FUNCTION: direct object of *understand* **(verstehen)**
  CASE: accusative
  SELECTION: neuter accusative → **es**

  Verstehen Sie das Buch? Ja, ich verstehe **es.**

CAREFUL – In English you choose the objective pronouns *him* or *her,* depending on the sex of the person you are referring to. In German, however, the gender of the pronoun is solely based on the grammatical gender of the noun being replaced. For example, neuter diminutives ending in **-chen** or **-lein** such as **das Mädchen** *(the young girl),* would be replaced by the neuter pronouns, **es** (accusative) or **ihm** (dative). Likewise **das Kind** *(the child)* which could refer to a person of any sex must be replaced by neuter pronouns according to its grammatical gender.

*Who helps the child? We are helping **her** (or **him**).*
ANTECEDENT: the child
GENDER: **das Kind** *(the child)* → neuter
FUNCTION: object of *help* (**helfen** takes a dative object)
CASE: dative
SELECTION: neuter dative → **ihm**

Wer hilft dem Kind? Wir helfen **ihm**.
dative object

STUDY TIPS
DIRECT AND INDIRECT OBJECT PRONOUNS

Flashcards

On the personal pronoun flashcards (p. 44), add sentences illustrating the pronoun's direct and indirect object forms. Underline the object pronouns; this will draw your attention to form changes, depending on the pronoun's function in the sentence.

er	he, it (subject)
Ich sehe ihn.	I see him/it. (direct object)
Ich gebe ihm das Buch.	I give him the book. (indirect object)
sie	they (subject)
Ich sehe sie.	I see them. (direct object)
Ich gebe ihnen das Buch.	I give them the book. (indirect object)

Pattern

① Look for similarities between direct object pronouns (accusative) and other parts of speech. Refer to the chart on p. 69.

What pattern do you see?

- 1st and 2nd pers. sing., **mich, dich,** the same initial letters **(m-, d-)** as possessive adjectives, **mein, dein** (Possessive adjectives, p. 132).
- 2nd pers. formal, **Sie,** and 3rd pers. pl., **sie,** the same as subject pronoun, (Subject pronouns, p. 46).
- 3rd pers. sing. and pl. direct object pronoun **(-n, -e, -s; e)** the same last letter as definite articles for direct objects, **den, die, das; die.** See chart p. 36.

② Look for similarities between direct object pronouns (accusative) and indirect object pronouns (dative), as well as other parts of speech.

What pattern do you see?

- 1st and 2nd pers. informal sing., **mir, dir:** direct object ending **–ch (mich, dich)** changes to **–r** in indirect object.
- 1st and 2nd pers. informal pl., **uns, euch:** same forms for direct and indirect object pronouns.
- 2nd pers. formal, **Sie, Sie, Ihnen,** and 3rd pers. plural, **sie, sie, ihnen:** same forms for subject, direct, and indirect pronouns, except for capitalization.
- 3rd pers. sing. and pl . indirect object pronoun last letter **(-m, -r, -m; -n):** the same last letter as definite articles for indirect objects, **dem, der, dem; den.**

Practice

1. Write a series of short German sentences with masculine, feminine, neuter, and plural direct objects. Rewrite the sentences replacing the direct object with the appropriate object pronoun.

   Ich kaufe die Blumen. *I buy the flowers.*
   Ich kaufe sie. *I buy them.*

2. Add an indirect object to the original sentences you created under 1 above. Rewrite the sentences replacing the indirect object with the appropriate object pronoun.

   Ich kaufe meiner Mutter die Blumen. *I buy my mother flowers.*
   Ich kaufe ihr die Blumen. *I buy her flowers.*

3. Replace both the direct and indirect objects with pronouns in the sentences you've created under 2. Refer to your textbook for the correct word order.

   Ich kaufe sie ihr. *I buy them for her.*

REVIEW ACTIVITY

Using the chart p. 69, indicate the information requested about the pronouns in bold.

a. I believe **you.**
   Person: 1st 2nd 3rd
   Number: singular plural

b. We saw **him** often.
   Person: 1st 2nd 3rd
   Number: singular plural

c. They called **her.**
   Person: 1st 2nd 3rd
   Number: singular plural

d. You already told **them.**
   Person: 1st 2nd 3rd
   Number: singular plural

19 WHAT IS A PREPOSITION?

A **PREPOSITION** is a word usually placed in front of a noun or pronoun showing the relationship between that noun or pronoun and other words in the sentence. The noun or pronoun following the preposition is called the **OBJECT OF THE PREPOSITION.** The preposition plus its object is called a **PREPOSITIONAL PHRASE.**

prepositional phrase

Jade has an appointment *after* school.

noun preposition object of preposition

19.1 IN ENGLISH

Prepositions normally indicate location, direction, time, manner, and relationships, such as causality *(because of, due to).*

- prepositions showing location or position

  Axel was *in* the car.
  Anna is sitting *behind* you.

- prepositions showing direction

  We went *to* school.
  The students came directly *from* class.

- prepositions showing time and date

  Many Germans go on vacation *in* August.
  Their son will be home *at* Christmas.
  I'm meeting him *before* 4:30 today.

- prepositions showing manner

  He writes *with* a pen.
  They left *without* us.

Other frequently used prepositions are: *during, since, between, of, about.* Some English prepositions are made up of more than a single word: *because of, in front of, instead of, due to, in spite of, on account of.*

An object of a preposition is a noun or pronoun that follows a preposition and is related to it. It answers the question *whom?* or *what?* asked after the preposition.

Franz is leaving without Effi.
Franz is leaving *without whom?* Without Effi.
Effi is the noun object of the preposition *without*.

The baby eats with a spoon.
The baby eats *with what?* With a spoon.
A spoon is the noun object of the preposition *with*.

When the object of the preposition is a pronoun, an object pronoun is used (Object of preposition pronouns, p. 80).

Johan goes out with her.

Johan goes out *with whom?* With her.
Her is the pronoun object of the preposition *with*.

19.2 IN GERMAN

Unlike in English, where the form of the noun or pronoun object is the same regardless of the preposition, in German the noun or pronoun object will be in the accusative, dative, or genitive case depending on the preposition. Be sure to learn the meaning and use of each German preposition, as well as the case that must follow it.

Below are examples of various prepositions, each requiring a different case.

- **durch** *(through)* → accusative object

  Er wirft den Ball **durch** das Fenster.
  (das: accusative)
  He throws the ball ***through*** *the window.*

- **bei** *(with)* → dative object

  Er wohnt **bei** seiner Tante.
  (seiner: dative)
  He lives ***with*** *his aunt.*

- **trotz** *(in spite of)* → genitive object

  Trotz des Regens machten wir einen Spaziergang.
  (des: genitive)
  In spite of *the rain we took a walk.*

TWO-WAY PREPOSITIONS

German also has a group of prepositions called **TWO-WAY PREPOSITIONS**, so called because they can be followed by either an accusative or a dative object depending on whether the preposition is used to indicate destination or location.

- when used with a verb expressing motion in a particular direction or from one position to another → accusative

  We are driving ***into*** *town tomorrow.*
  Driving in a particular direction → accusative
  Wir fahren morgen **in** die Stadt.
  (die: accusative object)

  He lays the book ***on*** *the table.*
  Book moved from one position to another → accusative
  Er legt das Buch **auf** den Tisch.
  (den: accusative object)

- when used with a verb expressing location or destination → dative

> *Do you live **in** the city?*
> Expressing location, no motion → dative
> Wohnt ihr **in** der Stadt?
> dative object
>
> *The book lies **on** the table.*
> Expressing location, no motion → dative
> Das Buch liegt **auf** dem Tisch.
> dative object

CAREFUL – When two-way prepositions are not used to distinguish between motion and location, the object goes in the case that always follows that specific preposition in combination with a specific verb. For example, in the verbal expression *to speak about,* **sprechen über,** the preposition **über** is followed by an object in the accusative case and in the verbal expression *to work on,* **arbeiten an,** the preposition **an** is followed by an object in the dative case.

19.3 POSITION OF A PREPOSITION AND ITS OBJECT

IN ENGLISH

In spoken English one often encounters **DANGLING PREPOSITIONS** referring to prepositions separated from their object, in particular in questions starting with *who, what, when,* etc. and in relative clauses (Relative pronouns, p. 162). Restructuring the questions and sentences so that the preposition is placed before its object, as in formal English, will help you identify prepositional phrases.

Spoken English	→	**Formal English**
Who did you get the book from?		*From whom* did you get the book?
object (*whom*) — dangling preposition		object of preposition *from*

IN GERMAN

There are no dangling prepositions. Nearly all German prepositions are placed as they are in formal English, that is, either before their object within the sentence or at the beginning of a question.

> ***Who** are you leaving **with?*** →
> ***With whom** are you leaving?*
> **Mit wem** gehst du?
> preposition + object
>
> ***Who** did you get the book **from?*** →
> ***From whom** did you get the book?*
> **Von wem** hast du das Buch bekommen?
> preposition + object

Your textbook will indicate the few prepositions that must or can be placed after their objects, such as **entlang: die Straße entlang** *(along the street)*, **gegenüber** *(across from)*, and a special use of **nach** *(according to)* when placed after the noun.

19.4 PREPOSITION OR SEPARABLE PREFIX?

The position of prepositions in German sentences enables us to distinguish when they are used as prepositions or separable prefixes (Prefixes, p. 12).

- if they are next to their object → prepositions

  Sie **arbeitet mit** meiner Mutter.
  preposition — object of preposition
  *She **works with** my mother.*

  Wir **gehen vor** dem Vochenende.
  preposition — object of preposition
  *We're **going before** the weekend.*

- if they are at the end of a clause or attached to a verb → separable prefixes

  Wer **kommt mit?**
  verb **mitkommen** (to come along)
  *Who is **coming along?***

  Das **kommt** manchmal **vor.**
  verb **vorkommen** (to happen)
  *That **happens** sometimes.*

CAREFUL – When you consult the dictionary to find the German equivalent of verb phrases such as "to talk about" "to look for" make sure to look for the entire phrase, not just the verb. For instance, do not stop at the first entry for talk or look and then add the German equivalent of *about* or *for.* Continue searching for the entire verb phrase: *to talk about* or *to look for* so that you will know if a preposition is needed in German and, if so, which one. In this case the German verb **sprechen** *(to talk)* is followed by the preposition **über** *(about)* and the German verb **suchen** *(to look for)* and **bezahlen** *(to pay for)* are not followed by prepositions.

*We **are talking about** politics.*
Wir **sprechen über** Politik.

*We **looked for** the book.*
Wir **suchten** das Buch.

*We **paid for** the meal.*
Wir **bezahlten** das Essen.

Here are additional examples.

English preposition	**German no preposition**
to pay *for*	bezahlen
to look *at*	betrachten
No preposition	**Preposition**
to answer	antworten **auf**
Change of preposition	
to wait *for*	warten **auf** *(on)*
to be interested *in*	interessieren **für** *(for)*

When your German textbook introduces phrases such as **warten auf** + accusative object *(to wait for)* and **bitten um** + accusative object *(to ask for)*, make sure to learn the verb together with the preposition and its case so that you can use the entire pattern correctly.

STUDY TIPS
PREPOSITIONS

Flashcards

1. Create a card for each preposition. On the German side, include the case (Acc., Dat., Acc./Dat., or Gen.) that follows that preposition. Add a sample sentence.

2. Sort the cards according to the case that follows. To remember the case, here are some strategies other learners have used:

   a. Preposition + accusative — Create a phrase or acronym based on the first letter of each preposition in the group: **bis, für, durch, gegen, um, ohne** "Barking, furry dogs greet us often" or the acronym "dogfub."

   b. Preposition + dative — Sing the prepositions aus, **außer, bei, mit, nach, seit, von, zu** to a familiar tune. For example: in alphabetical order to the tune of the *Blue Danube Waltz.*

   c. Two-way prepositions — Two suggestions:

      - Imagine all the places a housefly could fly or land in relation to an object, such as a wine glass: **über** *(above)*, **unter** *(below)*, **vor** *(in front of)*, **hinter** *(behind)*, **auf** *(on top of)*, **an** *(up against)*, **in** *(in)*, **neben** *(beside)*, **zwischen** *(between)*.

- Draw two related pictures. In the first picture, illustrate an object or person moving to a new location *(The cat crawls under a chair).* In the second picture, illustrate that object or person in a stationary position *(The cat is sleeping under the chair).* Under each picture, write the corresponding sentence in German using the correct preposition and case to describe the scene.

③ As you learn more prepositions that go with verbs, make sure that you write these phrases down with any relevant information. For example, **arbeiten** *(to work)* is a good start, but **arbeiten – arbeitete – hat gearbeitet** (Principal parts, p.79) is better, and adding **arbeiten an** + dative *(to work on something)* is even better.

REVIEW ACTIVITY

I. Circle the prepositions in the following sentences.

a. A mouse darted behind the table.

b. The letter was hidden under the papers.

c. We met at the museum in Stuttgart.

d. On Saturday let's look around the city.

e. They met promptly at 5 o'clock.

f. Certainly, we can do it without delay!

II. Restructure the dangling prepositions in the following sentences so that the structure in English will parallel the structure of a German sentence.

a. I can't tell what they're laughing about.

____

b. Who are you doing that for?

____

c. What place does he work at?

____

d. That's not really something I am interested in.

____

20 WHAT IS AN OBJECT OF PREPOSITION PRONOUN?

An **OBJECT OF PREPOSITION PRONOUN** is a pronoun used an object of a preposition.

> They went out with *me.*
> pronoun *me* object of preposition *with*

20.1 IN ENGLISH

Object of preposition pronouns are the same as the pronouns used as direct and indirect objects. They can replace any noun object, including persons, things, or ideas (Direct and indirect object pronouns, p. 68).

> The teacher saw *me.*
> direct object

> The teacher gave *me* the book.
> indirect object

> The teacher spoke with *me* after class.
> object of preposition *with*

> The teacher talked about *it* in class.
> object of preposition *about*

20.2 IN GERMAN

The objects of prepositions can be in the accusative, dative, or genitive case. Normally we replace a noun object with a pronoun only if the noun replaced refers to a person. A different construction is used when the pronoun refers to a thing or idea. Let us look at the two types of constructions.

REFERRING TO A PERSON

When the pronoun object of a preposition refers to a person or an animal, follow the steps you have already learned in order to choose the appropriate personal pronoun.

1. ANTECEDENT: Find the noun replaced.
2. GENDER: Determine the gender of the antecedent.
3. CASE: Identify the case required by the preposition.
4. SELECTION: Select the appropriate pronoun from from the chart on p. 68

The following are examples showing how to analyze sentences that have a pronoun referring to a person as the object of a preposition.

Is Anja buying something for her brother?
Yes, she is buying something ***for him.***

1. ANTECEDENT: brother
2. GENDER: **der Bruder** *(brother)* is masculine.
3. CASE: **für** takes an accusative object
4. SELECTION: masculine accusative → **ihn**

Kauft Anja etwas für ihren Bruder?
Ja, sie kauft etwas **für ihn.**

Did Franz talk about his sister?
No, he did not talk ***about her.***

1. ANTECEDENT: sister
2. GENDER: **die Schwester** *(sister)* is feminine.
3. CASE: **von** takes a dative object
4. SELECTION: feminine dative → **ihr**

Sprach Franz von seiner Schwester?
Nein, er sprach nicht **von ihr.**

REFERRING TO A THING

To replace a pronoun object of a preposition whose antecedent is a thing or idea, German uses a construction called the **DA-COMPOUND.** It is formed by adding the prefix **da-** to the preposition, or **dar-** if the preposition begins with a vowel.

Let us look at some examples.:

Does Beth talk ***about her courses?*** *Yes, she does talk* ***about them.***
Spricht Beth **von** **ihren Kursen?** Ja, sie spricht **davon.**

preposition	noun (a thing)	**da**-construction: **da-** + preposition **von**

Are you thinking ***about the price?*** *Don't think* ***about it.***
Denken Sie **an** **den Preis?** Denken Sie nicht **daran!**

preposition	noun (a thing)	**da**-construction: **da-** + **-r-** + preposition **an**

These **da**-compounds are not formed with every preposition. Your German textbook will discuss this construction and its use in greater detail.

CAREFUL – Be sure to look at an entire sentence, not just at the word itself, to establish its function. For example, **ihn** *(him* or *it)* could be the direct object form (accusative) of the masculine pronoun or the object of a preposition that takes the accusative case.

Da-compounds are similar to **wo**-compounds (see Interrogative pronouns, p. 142).

STUDY TIPS
OBJECT OF PREPOSITION PRONOUNS

Pattern

Let's compare **da-** to **wo-** -compounds to interrogative pronouns to find similarities in form and usage.

Compare forms

wo-compound	**da-compound**
woran	daran
worin	darin
wofür	dafür
womit	damit

Compare forms

Both used when anticipating or referring to a thing or an idea, not a person.

wo-compound in questions	**da-compound in statements**
Worauf wartest du?	
Wartest du ***auf den Bus?***	Nein, **darauf** warte ich nicht.
What *are you waiting* ***for?***	
Are you waiting ***for the bus?***	*No, I'm not waiting* ***for it.***

REVIEW ACTIVITY

The following English sentences contain prepositions and their objects written in italics.

I. Circle italicized nouns referring to persons.

II. Underline italicized nouns referring to things.

III. Indicate the type of construction you must use in German: preposition + personal pronoun (PP) or **da**-compound (**da**-C).

a. We're waiting for *Greg*.	PP	**da**-C
b. Thank you for the *present*!	PP	**da**-C
c. I wrote to *Emily*.	PP	**da**-C
d. We're looking forward to the *vacation*.	PP	**da**-C
e. Are you happy with the *situation*?	PP	**da**-C
f. I know nothing about my new *classmates*.	PP	**da**-C

WHAT ARE THE PRINCIPAL PARTS OF A VERB? 21

The **PRINCIPAL PARTS OF A VERB** are the forms needed in order to create all the different tenses (Tense p. 59; Past Tense, p. 102; Participles, p. 106).

Present	I eat
Present perfect	I have eaten
Past	I ate
Past perfect	I had eaten
Future	I will eat
Future perfect	I will have eaten

21.1 IN ENGLISH

The principal parts of an English verb are the infinitive *(to eat)*, the past tense *(ate)*, and the past participle *(eaten)*. If you know these parts, you can form all the other tenses by adding an auxiliary verb (Auxiliary verbs, p. 88).

English verbs fall into two categories, depending on how they form their principal parts.

REGULAR (WEAK) VERBS — These verbs are called regular because their past tense and past participle forms follow the predictable pattern of adding *-ed*, *-d*, or *-t* to the infinitive. They have two distinct principal parts: the infinitive and the past tense.

Infinitive	**Past tense/Past participle**
to walk	walk*ed*
to live	live*d*
to burn	burn*ed* (burn*t*)

IRREGULAR (STRONG) VERBS — These verbs are called irregular because their principal parts do not follow a regular pattern. They have three distinct principal parts: the infinitive, the past tense, and the past participle.

Infinitive	**Past tense**	**Past participle**
to sing	sang	sung
to draw	drew	drawn
to hit	hit	hit
to lie	lay	lain
to ride	rode	ridden

21.2 IN GERMAN

While English makes a distinction between regular and irregular verbs, German refers to a distinction between weak verbs and strong verbs depending on how they form their principal parts (Conjugation, p. 51).

WEAK (REGULAR) VERBS

Weak verbs resemble English regular verbs in that the stem of the principal parts of the verb doesn't change. They have three principal parts: the infinitive, the past tense given in the 3rd person singular, and the past participle.

1st principal part: infinitive	kochen	*to cook*
2nd principal part: past tense (3rd pers. sing.)	kochte	*cooked*
3rd principal part: past participle	gekocht	*cooked*

Unless the verb has an inseparable prefix, the various principal parts are formed by adding various prefixes and/or suffixes to the stem (Prefixes, p. 13).

- the past tense is formed by adding a **-t-** (or **-et-** if the verb stem ends in **-d** or **-t**) to the stem of the infinitive + the endings for the different persons.
- the past participle is usually formed by adding the prefix **ge-** and the suffix **-t** or **-et** to the stem of the infinitive.

	Infinitive	**Past tense**	**Past participle**
to make	machen	machte	gemacht
to work	arbeiten	arbeitete	gearbeitet

STRONG (IRREGULAR) VERBS

Strong verbs resemble English irregular verbs in that they have unpredictable principal parts. They have three principal parts: the infinitive, the past tense given in the 3rd person singular, and the past participle.

1st principal part: infinitive	finden	*to find*
2nd principal part: past tense (3rd pers. sing.)	fand	*found*
3rd principal part: past participle	gefunden	*found*

The irregularity of strong verbs is shown in a variety of ways:

- the vowel of the verb stem often changes in the past tense and in the past participle.
- the past tense endings are different than those for weak verbs.
- the past participle is usually formed by adding the prefix **ge-** and the ending **-en** or **-n.**

	1st Infinitive	**2nd Past tense**	**3rd Past participle**
to come	kommen	kam	**ge**komm**en**
to do	tun	tat	**ge**tan

Besides the irregularities listed above, other strong verbs show their irregularity in different ways:

Stem-changing verbs — These verbs have a fourth principal part: the 3rd person singular of the present tense reflecting the stem vowel change in the 2nd and 3rd person singular of the present tense.

1st principal part: infinitive	laufen	*to run*
2nd principal part: past tense (3rd pers. sing.)	lief	*ran*
3rd principal part: past participle	**ge**laufen	*run*
4th principal part: present tense (3rd pers. sing.)	läuft	*runs*

Here are a couple of examples of the four principal parts of stem-changing verbs.

	1st Infinitive	**2nd Past tense**	**3rd Past participle**	**4th Present tense**
to read	lesen	las	**ge**lesen	l**ie**st
to take	nehmen	nahm	**ge**nomm**en**	n**i**mmt

While these verbs are sometimes called irregular in German textbooks, they are better understood as belonging to groups of similar changes in the stem. Learning these groups will help you remember the patterns and learn the vowel changes of new verbs that follow them.

MIXED-VERBS

Your German textbook will show you how to form the principal parts of these verbs which have forms that follow the weak pattern and others the strong pattern. There are not many of them, but many are very common verbs. For example, **bringen** *(to bring)*, **denken** *(to think)*, **kennen** *(to know someone)*, and **wissen** *(to know something)*.

Most German dictionaries include an alphabetized list of irregular verbs with their principal parts. By memorizing the principal parts of verbs you will be able conjugate verbs properly in all their tenses.

STUDY TIPS
PRINCIPAL PARTS

When you learn a new strong verb, look for another strong verb that changes its vowels in the past tense and the past participle in the same way. Make your own lists of strong verbs according to the vowel pattern in the principal parts.

Infinitive	**Past tense**	**Past Participle**
-ei-	**-ie-**	**-ie-**
schr**ei**ben *(to write)*	schr**ie**b	geschr**ie**ben
bl**ei**ben *(to stay)*	bl**ie**b	gebl**ie**ben

Infinitive	**Past tense**	**Past Participle**
-i-	**-a-**	**-u-**
f**i**nden *(to find)*	f**a**nd	gef**u**nden
tr**i**nken *(to drink)*	tr**a**nk	getr**u**nken
-ie-	**-o-**	**-o-**
fl**ie**gen *(to fly)*	fl**o**g	gefl**o**gen
verl**ie**ren *(to lose)*	verl**o**r	verl**o**ren

Flashcard

① To review the principal parts of verbs, take out the flashcards you created to learn the meaning of verbs (Study tips, p. 55) and sort them into two groups: weak verbs and strong verbs. On the German side, write weak or strong and add the principal parts: infinitive, past, past participle.

(weak)	kaufen	kaufte	gekauft
(strong)	gehen	ging	gegangen

② Work with your flashcards in two ways:

a. Group the strong verbs according to the vowel patterns you determined above. Practice saying the pattern out loud for each verb in the group. Repeat the pattern until you can remember it without looking at the card.

b. Mix the strong and weak verbs together and go through the cards. As you practice forming the past participle, identify the verb as a weak or strong verb.
   - if weak, you need **–t** in the past participle.
   - if strong, you need **-en** in the past participle.
   - if strong, focus on the vowel pattern.
   - if there is a prefix, determine if it is separable or inseparable.
   - if separable, insert **–ge-** between the prefix and the stem.
   - if inseparable, no **ge-** is used.

REVIEW ACTIVITY

Indicate whether the following German verbs are weak, strong, or mixed.

a. kaufen	kaufte	gekauft	W	S	M
b. beginnen	begann	begonnen	W	S	M
c. rennen	rannte	gerannt	W	S	M
d. liegen	lag	gelegen	W	S	M
e. fragen	fragte	gefragt	W	S	M
f. sitzen	saß	gesessen	W	S	M
g. bringen	brachte	gebracht	W	S	M
h. falten	faltete	gefaltet	W	S	M

22 WHAT IS AN AUXILIARY VERB?

A verb is called an **AUXILIARY VERB** or **HELPING VERB** when it helps another verb, called the **MAIN VERB,** to form one of its tenses or alter its meaning.

He *has been gone* two weeks.	*has*	**auxiliary verb**
	been	**auxiliary verb**
	gone	**main verb**

A verb tense composed of an auxiliary verb + a main verb is called a **COMPOUND TENSE.** In a compound tense only the auxiliary verb is conjugated.

Julia *had studied* for the exam.
auxiliary verb (*had*) — main verb (*studied*)
compound tense

Julia *studies* for the exam.
simple tense

22.1 IN ENGLISH

There are three auxiliary verbs: *to have, to be,* and *to do.*

- auxiliary verbs are used to indicate the tense of the main verb.

  Jade *is reading* a book.
  auxiliary *to be* + present participle of *to read*
  present progressive (p. 61)

  Jade *has written* a book.
  auxiliary *to have* + past participle of *to write*
  present perfect (p. 99)

  Jade *does write* a book.
  auxiliary *to do* + infinitive
  present emphatic (p. 61)

- the auxiliary verb *to do* is used to help formulate questions (Interrogative, p. 158) and to make sentences negative (Negative, p. 155).

  Does Jade *read* a book?
  Jade *does not read* a book.

- the auxiliary verb *to be* is also used to indicate the verb is in the passive voice (Voice, p. 188).

  The book *is read* by many people.

MODALS — There is also a series of auxiliary verbs, called **MODALS,** such as *will, would, may, must, can, could,* that are used to change the tense or meaning of the main verb expressed in its infinitive form.

- the modal *will* is used to indicate the future tense (Future p. 99).

  Jade will read a book.
  modal *will* + infinitive *read*

- most modals are used to change the meaning of the main verb expressed in its infinitive form.

  Jade *may read* a book.
  Jade *must read* a book.
  Jade *can read* a book.

22.2 IN GERMAN

As in English, German has auxiliary verbs and modals.

AUXILIARY VERBS

The three main auxiliary verbs are **sein** *(to be)*, **haben** *(to have)*, and **werden** *(to become)*. As in English, auxiliary verbs are primarily used to indicate the tense of the main verb. In the examples below, notice that the conjugated auxiliary verb is in the second position of the sentence and the past participle (Participles, 106) or the infinitive form of the main verb (Verbs. 29) is at the end of the sentence.

- **sein** + past participle or **haben** + past participle → past tense (p. 99)

  Franz **hat** das Buch **gelesen**.
  auxiliary **haben** + past participle of **lesen** *(to read)* → present perfect
  *Franz **read** the book. [Franz **has read** the book.]*

  Franz **ist** zur Bibliothek **gegangen**.
  auxiliary **sein** + past participle of **gehen** *(to go)* → present perfect
  *Franz **went** to the library. [Franz **has gone** to the library.]*

It may help you to remember the German forms if you recognize that older forms of English, in Shakespeare for example, also used *to be* as an auxiliary verb with main verbs of motion or change of state in similar constructions, such as *the time is come*.

- **werden** + infinitive → future (p. 99)

  Franz **wird** das Buch **lesen.**
  auxiliary **werden** + infinitive of **lesen**
  *Franz **will read** the book.*

- **werden** + past participle → passive voice (p. 189)

  Das Buch **wird gelesen**.
  auxiliary **werden** + past participle of **lesen** → present passive voice
  *The book **is being read.***

22.2

MODALS

As in English, German has a series of modals that are used to change the tense or meaning of the main verb expressed in the infinitive form. German modals are verbs conjugated in the present and past tenses. The modal is in the second position of the sentence and the main verb in the infinitive form is at the end of the sentence.

- **können** *(to be able, can)*

  Lukas **kann** dieses Buch **lesen**.
  *Lukas **can read** this book.*
  [Lukas *has the ability to read* the book.]

- **dürfen** *(to be permitted to, may)*

  Lukas **darf** dieses Buch **lesen**.
  *Lukas **may read** this book.*
  [Lukas *is allowed to read* the book.]

- **müssen** *(to be obligated to, must)*

  Lukas **muss** dieses Buch **lesen**.
  *Lukas **must read** this book.*
  [Lukas *has to read* the book.]

- **sollen** *(to be supposed to, should)*

  Lukas **soll** dieses Buch **lesen**.
  *Lukas **should read** this book.*
  [Lukas *ought to read* the book.]

- **wollen** *(to want to)*

  Lukas **will** dieses Buch **lesen**.
  *Lukas **wants to read** this book.*

CAREFUL – Don't confuse **will**, the 1st and 3rd person singular form of the German modal verb **wollen** (*to want*), and the English modal *will* that puts the main verb in the future.

Ich **will** gehen. *I **want** to go.*	(**wollen** = *to want to* → **modal**)
Ich **werde** gehen. *I **will** go.*	(**werden** = *to become* → **auxiliary to form *future tense*)**

Consult your textbook for the meaning of German modal verbs and how they are used.

STUDY TIPS
AUXILIARY VERBS

Pattern

Compare the conjugation of modal verbs with the conjugation of regular and stem-changing verbs you learned previously.

Regular *wohnen* (to live)		**Stem-changing** *fahren* (to drive)		**Modal** *können* (to be able to, can)		**Modal** *müssen* (to have to, must)	
wohne	wohnen	fahre	fahren	kann	können	muss	müssen
wohnst	wohnt	fährst	fahrt	kannst	könnt	musst	müsst
wohnt	wohnen	fährt	fahren	kann	können	muss	müssen

What similarities and differences do you see?

- All verbs: 2nd per. sing. end with -st.
- All verbs: infinitive, 1st and 3rd pers. pl. identical forms.
- Modal verbs: 1st and 3rd pers. sing. identical.
- Vowel change: stem-changing verbs have a vowel change in 2nd and 3rd pers. sing. vs. modal verbs have a vowel change in the 1st, 2nd, and 3rd pers. sing.
- Endings: regular and stem-changing verbs have an ending in the 1st, 2nd, and 3rd pers. sing., vs. modal verbs have no ending in the 1st and 3rd pers. sing., only in the 2nd pers. sing.

Flashcards

Create a flashcard for each modal verb. On the German side, include the conjugation pattern and a sample sentence.

REVIEW ACTIVITY

Circle the auxiliary verbs and modals in the following English sentences.

I. Cross out the English auxiliaries that will not be expressed as auxiliaries in a German sentence.

II. On the line below indicate the verbs that will be expressed in a German sentence.

a. They are working on the problem.

____

b. We can go now.

____

c. You do have a point.

____

d. She has waited a long time.

____

e. He will arrive later.

____

f. Shall I do it again?

____

WHAT ARE REFLEXIVE PRONOUNS AND VERBS? 23

A **REFLEXIVE VERB** is a verb that is accompanied by a pronoun, called a **REFLEXIVE PRONOUN**, that serves *to reflect* the action of the verb back to the subject.

> subject = reflexive pronoun → the same person
>
> <u>She</u> <u>*cut herself*</u> with the knife.
> reflexive verb

23.1 IN ENGLISH

Many regular verbs can take on a reflexive meaning by adding a reflexive pronoun.

> The child *dresses* the doll.
> regular verb
>
> The child *dresses herself.*
> verb + reflexive pronoun

In some regional varieties of spoken English, many verbs are made reflexive with an object pronoun instead of a reflexive pronoun (Object pronouns, p. 68).

> I'll go get *me* a glass of water.
> object pronoun instead of reflexive pronoun *myself*

Reflexive pronouns end with *-self* in the singular and *-selves* in the plural.

	Subject pronoun	**Reflexive pronoun**
Singular		
1st person	I	myself
2nd person	you	yourself
3rd person	he	himself
	she	herself
	it	itself
Plural		
1st person	we	ourselves
2nd person	you	yourselves
3rd person	they	themselves

As the subject changes so does the reflexive pronoun, because they both refer to the same person or object.

> *I* cut *myself.*
> *Hans and Julia* blamed *themselves* for the accident.

Although the subject pronoun *you* is the same for the singular and plural, there is a difference in the reflexive pronouns: *yourself* (singular) is used when you are speaking to one person and *yourselves* (plural) is used when you are speaking to more than one.

Johan, did *you* make *yourself* a sandwich?
Children, make sure *you* wash *yourselves* properly.

Reflexive verbs can be in any tense in the active voice (Voice, p. 188): *I wash myself* (present), *I washed myself* (past), *I will wash myself* (future), etc. Reflexive pronouns can function as either direct objects *(I washed myself)*, indirect objects *(I made myself a sandwich)*, or objects of a preposition *(I worked on myself)*, but its form remains the same regardless of the function.

23.2 IN GERMAN

REFLEXIVE PRONOUNS

As in English, there is a different reflexive pronoun for each person. Since the reflexive pronoun can function as a direct object, indirect object, or object of a preposition, German reflexive pronouns have an accusative and dative use. As you can see in the chart below, the same form is used for accusative and dative reflexive pronouns, except for the 1st and 2nd persons singular.

Subject	**Reflexive**		
nominative	**accusative**	**dative**	
ich	mich	mir	*myself*
du	dich	dir	*yourself*
er sie es	sich	sich	*himself, herself, itself*
wir	uns	uns	*ourselves*
ihr	euch	euch	*yourselves*
sie	sich	sich	*themselves*
Sie	sich	sich	*yourself, yourselves*

Here are a few sentences illustrating the use of the accusative or dative reflexive pronoun, depending on its function, the verb and the preposition.

- as direct or indirect object of the verb

  *I cut **myself** with the knife.*
  direct object of *cut*
  Ich habe **mich** mit dem Messer geschnitten.
  accusative object of **geschnitten** *(to cut)*

  *You should write **yourself** a note.*
  indirect object of *write*
  You should write *to whom*? To yourself → indirect object
  Du solltest **dir** einen Zettel schreiben.
  dative object of **schreiben** *(to write)*

- as object of a preposition

He thinks only of ***himself****.*
object of preposition *of*
to think of → **denken an** + accusative
Er denkt nur an **sich**.
accusative object of **denken an**

You talk about ***yourself*** *too much.*
object of preposition *about*
to talk about → **reden von** + dative
Du redest zuviel von **dir**.
dative object of **von**

Pay special attention to verbs that take a direct object in English but require the dative case in German. These so-called dative verbs take a reflexive pronoun in the dative case (Objects, p. 64).

I can't help ***myself.***
direct object of help
Remember: to help → **helfen** + dative
Ich kann **mir** nicht helfen.
dative object of **helfen**

REFLEXIVE VERBS

Unlike English where the meaning of a regular verb can be changed by adding a reflexive pronoun, German has a series of verbs, called **REFLEXIVE VERBS**, whose meaning can only be conveyed with a reflexive pronoun. The English equivalents of these verbs do not have reflexive pronouns. Reflexive verbs are listed in the dictionary with the 3rd person reflexive pronoun **sich** + the infinitive.

sich erholen	*to recover*
sich befinden	*to be located*
sich verlieben	*to fall in love*

As in English, German reflexive verbs are conjugated in the various persons followed by a reflexive pronoun. Look at the present tense conjugation of **sich erholen** *(to recover)* that takes an accusative object.

Singular		
1st person	ich erhole mich	*I recover*
2nd person familiar	du erholst dich	*you recover*
	er erholt sich	*he, it recovers*
3rd person	sie erholt sich	*she, it recovers*
	es erholt sich	*it recovers*

Plural

1st person	wir erholen uns	*we recover*
2nd person familiar	ihr erholt euch	*you recover*
3rd person	sie erholen sich	*they recover*
2nd person formal	Sie erholen sich	*you recover*

As in English, reflexive verbs can be conjugated in all tenses. The subject pronoun and reflexive pronoun remain the same; only the verb form changes: ***du*** **erholst** ***dich*** (present), ***du*** **wirst** ***dich*** **erholen** (future), ***du*** **hast** ***dich*** **erholt** (perfect).

As you learn a new German verb, make sure to note the relationship between the verb and reflexive pronouns. Possible situations include:

- verbs that require a reflexive pronoun as part of the whole verb phrase

    Ich **freue mich** auf den Sommer **(sich freuen).**
    *I **look forward** to the summer.*

- verbs that can be used with or without a relative pronoun depending on the object

    Er **wäscht sich (sich waschen).**
    *He **bathes himself.***

    Sie **wäscht** ihr Auto **(waschen).**
    She ***washes*** *her car.*

- verbs that have a different meaning when they are reflexive.

    Wir **haben** uns an ihn **erinnert (sich erinnern).**
    *We **remembered** him.*

    Er **hat** uns an seinen Bruder **erinnert (erinnern).**
    *He **reminded** us of his brother.*

Your German textbook will introduce you to the various types of verbs and their English equivalent.

23.3 RECIPROCAL ACTION

English uses a regular verb followed by the expression "each other" to express reciprocal action, that is, an action between two or more persons or things.

The dog and the cat looked at *each other*.
The expression "each other" tells us that the action of *looking* was reciprocal, i.e., the dog looked at the cat and the cat looked at the dog.

Our children call *each other* every day.

The expression "each other" tells us that the action of *calling* is reciprocal, i.e., the various children call one another every day.

Since reciprocal verbs require that more than one person or thing be involved, the verb is always plural.

IN GERMAN

German usually uses reflexive pronouns to express an action that is reciprocal.

Wir **sehen uns** morgen.
*We'll **see each other** tomorrow.*

Unsere Kinder **rufen sich** jeden Tag an.
*Our children **call each other** every day.*

When it is not clear whether the reflexive pronoun refers to multiple subjects individually or reciprocally between them, the word **einander** "each other" can be used.

Sie lieben **sich**.
multiple subjects
or reciprocal
*They love **themselves.*** OR *They love **each other.***

Sie lieben **einander**.
reciprocal
*They love **each other.***

STUDY TIPS
REFLEXIVE PRONOUNS AND VERBS

Flashcards

Create flashcards for reflexive verbs. On the German side, include **sich** and the infinitive form of the verb and indicate the case of the reflexive pronoun. Finally, write two sample sentences in the first and third person singular.

sich interessieren + für *to be interested in something* (acc.)

Ich interessiere mich für Schach.
I'm interested *in chess.*

Sie interessiert sich für Sport.
She is interested *in sports.*

Practice writing reflexive (or reciprocal) and non-reflexive uses of verbs that can function in both ways.

Wir sehen den Film morgen. — not reflexive
We'll watch *the film tomorrow.*

Wir sehen uns morgen. — reflexive (reciprocal)
We'll see each other *tomorrow.*

REVIEW ACTIVITY

I. Fill in the proper reflexive pronoun in English.

a. Ruby, you should feel free to make________________at home.
b. We bought________________a new car.
c. The man hurt________________while changing the tire.
d. She taught________________to play the guitar.
e. I blame________________for the mistake.
f. Maura and Steve, you should get________________ready.

II. Using the sample conjugation on p. 96, fill in the accusative reflexive pronouns of the reflexive verb *sich freuen über* (to be happy about something).

ich freue ____________
du freust ____________
er/sie/es freut ____________
wir freuen ____________
ihr freut ____________
sie/Sie freuen ____________

WHAT IS THE FUTURE TENSE? 24

The **FUTURE TENSE** indicates that the action of the verb will take place some time in the future.

> I *will return* the book as soon as I can.
> future

24.1 IN ENGLISH

There are three ways of indicating an action to take place in the future.

- with the future tense: auxiliary *will* or *shall* + the dictionary form of the main verb. In conversation *will* and *shall* are often shortened to *'ll*. The time the future action will occur may or may not be indicated.

  > Axel *will do* his homework after supper.
  > (future tense plus a future time expression)
  >
  > I'*ll take* my umbrella because it will rain.
  > (future tense only)

- using in the present tense with an adverb (Adverbs, p. 165) or an expression of future time

  > Max *is meeting* Axel *tomorrow*.
  > present progressive — adverb
  >
  > Johan *goes* to Berlin *next week*.
  > present — expression of future time

- using the expression "going to" + infinitive of verb

  > Anna *is going to eat* later.
  > Are you *going to join* her?

24.2 IN GERMAN

There are two ways of indicating an action to take place in the future:

- with the future tense, **das Futur**: auxiliary verb **werden** *(to become)* conjugated to agree with the subject + the infinitive of the main verb which remains unchanged. The time of the future action may or may not be indicated.

  > Lukas und Max **werden** ihre Hausaufgabe **schreiben**.
  > werden: 3rd pers. pl. — schreiben: infinitive
  > *Lukas and Max* ***will write*** *their homework.*
  >
  > Ich **werde** heute Abend **ausgehen**.
  > werde: 2nd pers. sing., 2nd position — ausgehen: infinitive, end of sentence
  > **I *shall go out*** *tonight.*

- using in the present tense with an adverb or an expression of future time

> Hans und Lukas **schreiben morgen** ihre Prüfung.
> present + adverb of future time
> *Hans and Lukas* ***are writing*** *their test* ***tomorrow.***
>
> Er **fliegt nächstes Jahr** nach Deutschland.
> present + expression of future time
> *He* ***is flying*** *to Germany* ***next year.***

CAREFUL – Be sure to distinguish the various forms of the verb **werden** used as an auxiliary to form the future tense in German from the various forms of the modal German verb **wollen** *(to want)* which do not indicate the future (Auxiliary verbs, p. 89).

24.3 FUTURE OF PROBABILITY

In addition to expressing an action that will take place in the future, the future tense in German can be used to express a probable fact, or what the speaker feels is probably true. This is called the **FUTURE OF PROBABILITY.**

The idea of probability is expressed with words such as *must, probably, wonder.*

> My keys *must* be around here.
> My keys are *probably* around here.
> I *wonder* if my keys are around here.

IN GERMAN

Unlike English that uses the present tense, the idea of probability in German is usually expressed in the future tense accompanied with words such as **wohl** *(probably)*, **sicher** *(surely)*, and **vielleicht** *(perhaps)*.

> Meine Schlüsel **werden wohl** irgendwo hier **liegen**.
> my keys **will** probably around here **lie**
> adverb **(wohl)** + future tense of **liegen** *(to lie)*
> *My keys* ***are probably*** *around here.*
> present tense + present tense of ***to be***
>
> Sie **werden** dieses Buch **sicher kennen**.
> you **will** this book **surely know**
> adverb **(sicher)** + future tense of **kennen** *(to know)*
> *You* ***surely know*** *this book.*
> adverb + present tense of ***to know***

Other ways of expressing probability without the future tense may be covered in your textbook under subjective uses of modal verbs.

REVIEW ACTIVITY

In the sentences below underline the verbs in future tense. Circle the verbs in the present tense which are used with an expression of future time.

a. Next week we are going on vacation.

b. Erica will go downtown.

c. I shall return.

d. Tomorrow I am flying to Europe.

e. He's coming soon.

f. Will she return after the break?

25 WHAT IS THE PAST TENSE?

The **PAST TENSE** indicates that the action of the verb occurred in the past.

I *saw* you yesterday.

25.1 IN ENGLISH

There are several verb forms that indicate the past tense.

I worked	Simple past
I was working	Past progressive
I used to work	Habitual past (with helping verb *used to*)
I did work	Past emphatic
I have worked	Present perfect
I had worked	Past perfect

The simple past is a simple tense; that is, it consists of one word, *worked* in the example above. The other past tenses are compound tenses; that is, they consist of more than one word, an auxiliary plus a main verb, *was working, did work* in the example above (Auxiliary verbs, p. 86). In spoken English, the two tenses are often interchangeable.

SIMPLE PAST — There are two ways to form the simple past. If the verb is regular, the ending *–ed* (or *-d)* is added. If the verb is irregular, vowel and/or consonant changes are common.

Regular			**Irregular**
work	work*ed*	sing	s*a*ng
live	live*d*	see	s*aw*

PRESENT PERFECT — The present perfect is formed with the auxiliary to have in the present tense + the past participle of the main verb (Present, p. 61; Participles, p. 107).

I *have* *worked*.
present — past participle of *to work*

I *have* *seen* that film.
present — past participle of *to see*

25.2 IN GERMAN

There are two tenses commonly used to express an action in the past: the simple past and the present perfect. A third past tense, the past perfect (Past perfect, p. 112), has a more specific context.

Simple past – The simple past, **das Imperfekt** or **das Präteritum,** consists of only one word, formed differently depending if there is a change in spelling of the stem of the verb or not.

- stem with no change in spelling (weak verb) + the simple past marker **(-t-)** + an ending

  Ich **wohnte** in Hannover.
  verb stem **wohn**- + ending **-t-** + 1st person singular ending
  *I **lived** in Hanover.*

  Du **wohntest** in Hanover.
  verb stem **wohn-** + **-t-** + 2nd person singular ending
  *You **lived** in Hanover.*

- stem with a change in spelling (strong verb) + an ending

  Du **schwammst** jeden Tag.
  verb stem **schwamm- (schwimmen,** *to swim)* + 2nd person singular ending
  *You **swam** every day.*

  Wir **schwammen** jeden Tag.
  verb stem **schwamm**- + 1st person plural ending
  *We **swam** every day.*

The formation of the simple past depends on whether the verb is a strong or a weak verb (Conjugation, p. 51). Both the spelling of the verb stem and the endings may be affected. Your German textbook will explain in detail the formation of the simple past.

Present perfect — The present perfect tense, **das Perfekt,** is a compound tense, consisting of two parts: the auxiliary verbs **haben** *(to have)* or **sein** *(to be)* conjugated in the present tense + the past participle of the main verb. You must memorize which verbs require **haben** and which require **sein** as the auxiliary.

Ich **habe** in Hannover **gewohnt.**

present tense auxiliary **haben**	past participle main verb **wohnen** *(to live)*

*I **have lived** in Hanover. [**I've lived** in Hanover.]*

Ich **bin** jeden Tag **geschwommen.**

present tense auxiliary **sein**	past participle of main verb **schwimmen** *(to swim)*

*I **have swum** every day. [**I've swum** every day.]*

Some verbs can be used with either auxiliary depending on whether they take an object **(haben)** or not **(sein).**

Ich **bin** jeden Tag **gefahren**.
present tense auxiliary **sein** — past participle of main verb **fahren** (*to drive*)
***I have driven** every day. [**I've driven** every day.]*

Haben Sie mal einen BMW **gefahren?**
present tense auxiliary **haben** — object — past participle of main verb **fahren** (*to drive*)
***Have** you ever **driven** a BMW?*

In both English and German, the present perfect and the simple past have equivalent meanings. Their difference is one of style and usage: generally, the present perfect is used in conversation, whereas the simple past is more common in certain kinds of writing. Consult your textbook for more information.

STUDY TIPS

PAST TENSE

Pattern

Compare the conjugation of weak and strong verbs in the present and the past tense.

WEAK VERB
wohnen (*to live*)

	Present		Past
Singular			
1st	wohne	1st/3rd	wohnte
2nd	wohnst	2nd	wohntest
3rd	wohnt		
Plural			
1st/3rd	wohnen	1st/3rd	wohnten
2nd	wohnt	2nd	wohntet

STRONG/STEM CHANGE VERB
fahren (*to drive*)

	Present		Past
Singular			
1st	fahre	1st/3rd	fuhr
2nd	fährst	2nd	fuhrst
3rd	fährt		
Plural			
1st/3rd	fahren	1st/3rd	fuhren
2nd	fahrt	2nd	fuhrt

What similarities and differences do you see?

Endings:

- all verbs and tenses: 1st and 3rd pers. pl. are the same.
- strong and weak verbs past tense: 1st and 3rd pers. sing. are the same.
- strong verbs past tense: 1st and 3rd pers. sing. no ending; other endings same as in present tense.
- weak verbs past tense: all forms insert a **-t-** or **-te-** before the ending.

Vowel change:

- weak verbs: no vowel change from present to past.
- stem-changing verbs: stem vowel change in present tense occurs only in the 2nd and 3rd pers. sing.
- strong verbs: stem vowel change in past tense occurs in all forms.

REVIEW ACTIVITY

Underline the verb form(s) in the following sentences. Indicate whether the verb is in the simple past (SP) or the present perfect (PP).

a.	Last summer I went to Germany with my family.	SP	PP
b.	My mother has visited Germany many times.	SP	PP
c.	Our trip was fun and interesting.	SP	PP
d.	We travelled around for two weeks.	SP	PP
e.	I have shown my vacation photos to my German class.	SP	PP
f.	They've never seen some of the locations in the photos before.	SP	PP

26 WHAT IS A PARTICIPLE?

A **PARTICIPLE** is a form of a verb that can be used in one of two ways: with an auxiliary verb to indicate certain tenses or as an adjective to describe something.

> He *has closed* the door.
> auxiliary + participle → past tense
>
> He heard me through the *closed* door.
> participle describing *door* → adjective

There are two types of participles: the present participle and the past participle.

26.1 PRESENT PARTICIPLE

IN ENGLISH

The present participle is easy to recognize because it is the *-ing* form of the verb: *working, studying, dancing, playing.*

The present participle has three primary uses:

- as the main verb in compound tenses with the auxiliary verb *to be* (Auxiliary verbs, p. 88)

  > She *is writing* with her new pen.
  > present progressive of *to write*
  >
  > They *were sleeping.*
  > past progressive of *to sleep*

- as an adjective (Adjectives, p. 116)

  > Jade is a *loving* daughter.
  > describes the noun *daughter*
  >
  > He woke the *sleeping* child.
  > describes the noun *child*

- in a phrase (Sentences, p. 144)

  > *Turning the corner,* Tony ran into a tree.
  > participial phrase describing *Tony*

IN GERMAN

The present participle is always formed by adding **-d** to the infinitive.

Infinitive	Present participle
singen	singen**d**
spielen	spielen**d**
sprechen	sprechen**d**

Unlike English where present participles are used as part of the main verb and in participial phrases, in German they are used as adjectives with adjective endings.

> eine **liebende** Tochter
> *a **loving** daughter*
>
> das **schlafende** Kind
> *the **sleeping** child*

CAREFUL – Never assume that an English word ending with **-ing** is translated by its German counterpart ending in **-d.** The English progressive tenses formed with an auxiliary + present participle (she *is singing*, they *were dancing*) do not exist in German. These tenses are expressed by a one-word German verb whose tense corresponds to the tense of the English auxiliary.

> *She **is singing.***
> present progressive
>
> Sie **singt**.
> present
>
> *They **were dancing.***
> past progressive
>
> Sie **tanzten**.
> simple past

26.2 PAST PARTICIPLE

IN ENGLISH

The past participle is formed differently, depending on whether the verb is weak or strong (Conjugation, p. 51). It is the form of the verb that follows the various forms of the auxiliary *to have*: I *have spoken (strong)*, he *has written (strong)*, we *have walked (weak)*.

The past participle has three primary uses:

- as the main verb in perfect tenses with the auxiliary verb *to have* (Past, 102; Past perfect, p. 112; Future perfect, p. 114),

  > I *have written* all that I have to say.
  > present perfect of *to write*
  >
  > He *hadn't spoken* to me all day.
  > past perfect of *to speak*

- as the main verb in the passive voice with the auxiliary verb *to be* (Voice, p. 188)

  > That language *is* no longer *spoken*.
  > present passive
  >
  > That book *was written* last year.
  > past passive

- as an adjective

Is the *written* word more important than the *spoken* word?
describes the noun *word* — describes the noun *word*

The past participle is formed differently depending on whether the verb is weak or strong. While all weak verbs form their past participle according to the same rule, strong verbs have past participles that must be memorized, and mixed verbs share both features.

WEAK VERBS — When the verb has no prefix or a separable prefix, the past participles of weak verbs are formed by adding the prefix **ge-** and the suffix **-t** to the stem of the infinitive.

Infinitive	**Stem**	**Past participle**	
machen	mach-	**ge**mach**t**	*made*
glauben	glaub-	**ge**glaub**t**	*believed*

STRONG VERBS — The past participles of strong verbs often change the stem vowel, and occasionally some of the consonants. When the verb has no prefix or a separable prefix, the prefix **ge-** and the ending **-en** or **-n** are added to the stem.

Infinitive	**Past participle**	
schlafen	**ge**schlaf**en**	*slept*
gehen	**ge**gang**en**	*gone*
tun	**ge**ta**n**	*done*
liegen	**ge**leg**en**	*lain*

MIXED VERBS — The past participles of mixed verbs share the **ge-** and **-t** frame of weak verbs and add vowel changes and/or consonant changes shared by strong verbs. These verbs are few in number but used frequently.

Infinitive	**Past participle**	
kennen	**ge**kann**t**	*known*
bringen	**ge**brach**t**	*bought*
wissen	**ge**wuss**t**	*known*

Weak, strong, and mixed verbs with an inseparable prefix do not add the prefix **ge-** and verbs with a separable prefix add **ge-** between the prefix and the stem (Prefixes, p. 13).

Inseparable	**be**suchen	besuchte	besucht	*to visit*
Separable	**aus**suchen	suchte...aus	aus**ge**sucht	*to choose*
Inseparable	**be**kommen	bekam	bekommen	*to receive*
Separable	**mit**kommen	kam...mit	mit**ge**kommen	*to come along*
Inseparable	**ver**bringen	verbrachte	verbracht	*to spend (time)*
Separable	**mit**bringen	brachte...mit	mit**ge**bracht	*to bring along*

As in English, the past participle can be used in the perfect tenses, in the passive, and as an adjective.

- as the main verb in the perfect tenses: **haben** *(to have)* or **sein** *(to be)* + the past participle

  Ich **habe** das Buch **gelesen.**
  *I **have read** the book. [I **read** the book.]*

  Ich **bin** nach Hause **gekommen.**
  *I **have come** home. [I **came** home.]*

- as the main verb in the passive voice: **werden** *(to become)* + the past participle

  Das Buch **wird** von vielen Studenten **gelesen.**
  *The book **is read** by many students.*

- as an adjective with adjective endings

  Ich lese den **getippten** Brief.
  *I read the **typed** letter.*

Since there is no way to predict the vowel change in the past participle of a strong or mixed verb, you will have to memorize it when you learn the verb.

26.3 PRESENT PARTICIPLE VS GERUND

A **VERBAL NOUN**, also called a **GERUND**, is the form of a verb that functions as a noun in a sentence: it can be a subject, a direct object, an indirect object, or an object of a preposition.

It is important that you learn to distinguish an English participle from a gerund since German gerunds differ in form from present participles.

GERUND — A word ending in *-ing* is a gerund if you can use the interrogative pronoun *what* to replace it in a question. The gerund will answer this question.

Reading can be fun.
What can be fun? Reading.
Reading, a noun derived from the verb *to read,* is the subject of the sentence.

We have often thought about *moving.*
We have often thought about *what?* Moving.
Moving, a noun derived from the verb *to move,* is the object of the preposition *about.*

26.3

Present participle — A word ending in *-ing* is a present participle if you must use the verb *to do* to replace it in a question. The present participle will answer this question.

We are *reading*.
What *are we doing*? Reading.
Reading, the present participle of the verb *to read*, is part of the compound verb tense.

The family is *moving* next week.
What *is the family doing*? Moving.
Moving, the present participle of the verb *to move*, is part of the compound verb tense.

IN GERMAN

Gerunds are usually expressed by a neuter noun made from the infinitive of the verb.

lesen	→	**das** Lesen	*to read, reading*
singen	→	**das** Singen	*to sing, singing*

As you can see in the examples below, knowing how to distinguish a gerund from a present participle will enable you to select the correct form for German.

Talking *is silver,* ***being silent*** *is gold.* ["Silence is golden."]
What is silver? Talking.
What is gold? Being silent.
Talking and *being silent* are gerunds.
Reden ist Silber, **Schweigen** ist Gold.
(Reden: gerund; ist: verb; Schweigen: gerund; ist: verb)

We ***are talking*** *a lot.*
What are we doing? Talking.
Talking is a present participle used in the present tense.
Wir **reden** viel.
(reden: verb)

In German it is easy to distinguish a gerund from a conjugated verb. Since gerunds are nouns they are always capitalized, while verbs are not.

STUDY TIPS
PARTICIPLES

Flashcards

When you create flashcards for verbs, it is helpful to add the auxiliary verb associated with the past participle and memorize the principal parts (p. 84) with this addition.

sein	war	ist gewesen	*(to be)*
essen	aß	hat gegessen	*(to eat)*

REVIEW ACTIVITY

Circle the tense of the verb forms in italics: present participle (P) or past participle (PP).

a.	At 10:00 p.m. John was watching TV.	P	PP
b.	We had already gone when Tom called.	P	PP
c.	An antique dealer near our house fixes broken china.	P	PP
d.	Mary is studying in the library right now.	P	PP
e.	Prying eyes are everywhere in a spy film.	P	PP
f.	Many ships have sunk near that reef.	P	PP

27 WHAT IS THE PAST PERFECT TENSE?

The **PAST PERFECT TENSE,** also called the **PLUPERFECT,** indicates that the action of the verb was completed in the past before another action or event in the past.

> They *had* already *gone* by the time I arrived.
> past perfect — simple past
> 1 — 2
> Both actions 1 and 2 occurred in the past, but action 1 preceded action 2. Therefore, action 1 is in the past perfect.

27.1 IN ENGLISH

The past perfect is formed with the past tense auxiliary *had* + the past participle of the main verb: *I had walked, he had seen,* etc. (Participles, p. 107). In conversation, *had* is often shortened to *'d.*

Verb tenses indicate the time that an action occurs; therefore, when verbs in the same sentence are in the same tense, the actions took place at the same time. To show that actions took place at different times, different tenses must be used.

Look at the following examples.

> The mother *was crying* because her son *was leaving*.
> past progressive — past progressive
> 1 — 1
> Action 1 and action 2 took place at the same time.

> The mother *was crying* because her son *had left.*
> past progressive — past perfect
> 1 — 2
> Action 2 took place before action 1.

27.2 IN GERMAN

The past perfect, **das Plusquamperfekt,** is formed with the auxiliary verb **haben** *(to have)* or **sein** *(to be)* in the simple past tense + past participle of the main verb (p. 102; Past participle p. 107)). This is the same structure as in English with the addition of **sein** as an auxiliary. Note the order of the verb parts: in the 2nd position, the conjugated past tense of the auxiliary and, at the end of the sentence, the past participle of the main verb.

> Wir **hatten** den Film schon **gesehen**.
> simple past of **haben** *(to have)* auxiliary in 2nd position — past participle of **sehen** *(to see)* main verb at end of sentence
> *We **had** already **seen** the film.*

> Wir **waren** schon ins Kino **gegangen**.
> simple past of **sein** *(to be)* auxiliary in 2nd position — past participle of **gehen** *(to go)* main verb at end of sentence
> *We **had** already **gone** to the movies.*

Generally, the German past perfect is used the same way as the past perfect in English: to express an action or condition that ended before some other past action or condition that may or may not be stated. Notice how we can express the sequence of events by using different tenses.

Verb tense		**Time action takes place**
Present	0	now
Perfect or simple past	-1	before 0
Past perfect	-2	before -1

Here is an example:

*They **had** already **left** when I **arrived**.*
Sie **waren** schon **abgefahren**, als ich **ankam**.
past perfect -2 simple past -1

CAREFUL – You cannot always rely on spoken English to determine when to use the past perfect in German. In conversation, if it is clear which action came first, English sometimes uses the simple past to describe an action that preceded another.

Anja *forgot* (that) she *saw* that movie.
simple past simple past

Anja *forgot* (that) she *had seen* the movie.
simple past past perfect

Although the two sentences above mean the same thing, only the sequence of tenses in the second sentence would be correct in German.

Gabi **hat vergessen**, dass sie den Film **gesehen hatte**.
past perfect -1 past perfect -2

Both actions took place some time in the past. In German, the action of point -2 has to be in the past perfect because it took place before the action of point -1.

28 WHAT IS THE FUTURE PERFECT TENSE?

The **FUTURE PERFECT TENSE** indicates that the action of the verb will occur in the future before another action or event in the future.

> By the time we leave, he *will have finished.*
> future event — 2; future perfect — 1
>
> Both actions 1 and 2 will occur at some future time, but action 1 will be completed before action 2 takes place. Therefore, action 1 is in the future perfect tense.

> I won't meet him. I *will have left* before he arrives.
> future perfect — 1; future event — 2
>
> Both action 1 and event 2 will occur at some future time, but action 1 will be completed before a specific event in the future. Therefore, action 1 is in the future perfect tense.

28.1 IN ENGLISH

The future perfect is formed with the future auxiliary verb *will* + the present perfect tense (Past, p. 102), which consists of the auxiliary *have* + the past participle of the main verb: *I will have walked, she will have gone* (Participles, p. 107). In conversation *will* is often shortened to *'ll.*

The future perfect is often used following expressions such as *by then, by that time, by* + a date.

> By the end of the month, he*'ll have graduated.*
> By June, I*'ll have saved* enough to buy a car.

28.2 IN GERMAN

Like in English, the future perfect, **das Futur II,** is formed with the future auxiliary verb **werden** (Future, p. 99), which consists of the auxiliary **haben** *(to have)* or **sein** *(to be)* + past participle of the main verb.

> Wir **werden** den Film **gesehen haben**.
> past paticiple of **sehen** *(to see)*
> + infinitive of auxiliary **haben**
> future tense of **haben**
>
> *We **will have seen** the film.*

Note the order of the verb parts: in the 2nd position, the conjugated future tense of the auxiliary and, grouped together at the end of the sentence, the past participle of the main verb followed by its auxiliary in the infinitive

Generally, the German future perfect is used the same way as the future perfect in English: to express an action that will be completed in the future before some other future action or event, which may or may not be stated. Notice how we can express the sequence of events by using different tenses.

Verb tense		**Time action takes place**
Present	0	now
Future perfect	1	after 0 and before 2
Future	2	after 0 and after 1

Here is an example.

*They **will have left** before I arrive.*
Sie **werden abgefahren sein,** bevor ich ankomme.

future perfect — event in the future

1 — 2

Both actions will take place some time in the future. In German, the action of point 1 has to be in the future perfect because it will take place before the event of point 2.

29 WHAT IS AN ADJECTIVE?

An **ADJECTIVE** is a word that describes a noun or a pronoun. There are different types of adjectives; they are classified according to the way they describe a noun or pronoun.

DESCRIPTIVE ADJECTIVE — A descriptive adjective indicates a quality; it tells what kind of noun it is (p. 117).

> She read an *interesting* book.
> He has *brown* eyes.

POSSESSIVE ADJECTIVE — A possessive adjective shows possession; it tells whose noun it is (p. 131).

> *His* book is lost.
> *Our* parents are away.

INTERROGATIVE ADJECTIVE — An interrogative adjective asks a question about a noun (p. 136).

> *What* book is lost?
> *Which* book did you read?

DEMONSTRATIVE ADJECTIVE — A demonstrative adjective points out a noun (p. 145).

> *This* teacher is excellent.
> *That* question is very appropriate.

29.1 IN ENGLISH

English adjectives usually do not change their form, regardless of the noun or pronouns described.

29.2 IN GERMAN

While English adjectives do not change their form, German adjectives change in order to agree with the case, gender, and number of the noun they modify. The various types of adjectives are discussed in separate sections.

WHAT IS A DESCRIPTIVE ADJECTIVE? 30

A **DESCRIPTIVE ADJECTIVE**, also called a **QUALITATIVE ADJECTIVE**, is a word that indicates a quality of a noun or pronoun. As the name implies, it *describes* the noun or pronoun.

> The book is *interesting.*
> book: noun described — interesting: descriptive adjective

> It is *interesting.*
> It: pronoun described — interesting: descriptive adjective

30.1 IN ENGLISH

A descriptive adjective does not change form, regardless of the noun or pronoun it modifies.

> Children are *intelligent.*
> Children: noun described — intelligent: adjective

> She is an *intelligent* person.
> She: pronoun described — intelligent: adjective

The form of the adjective *intelligent* remains the same although the persons described are different in number: *children* is plural and *person* is singular.

Descriptive adjectives are divided into two groups depending on how they are connected to the noun they modify.

PREDICATE ADJECTIVES — Predicate adjectives are connected to the noun they describe, always the subject of the sentence, by **LINKING VERBS** such as *to be, to feel, to look* (Predicate nouns, p. 48).

> The children are *good.*
> children: noun described — are: linking verb — good: predicate adjective

> The house looks *small.*
> house: noun described — looks: linking verb — small: predicate adjective

Attributive adjectives — Attributive adjectives describe a noun without a linking verb and always precede it.

The *good* children were praised.
attributive adjective — noun described

The family lives in a *small* house.
attributive adjective — noun described

30.2 IN GERMAN

As in English, descriptive adjectives can be identified as predicate or attributive adjectives. While predicate adjectives do not take any endings, attributive adjectives do.

PREDICATE ADJECTIVES

Predicate adjectives have the same form as the dictionary entry for the adjective, regardless of the gender and number of the nouns or pronouns they modify.

*The chairs are **small**.*
Die Stühle sind **klein**.
masculine plural

*The house is **small.***
Das Haus ist **klein.**
neuter singular

ATTRIBUTIVE ADJECTIVES

Attributive adjectives can have **WEAK, STRONG**, or **MIXED ENDINGS** depending on the the type of word which precedes them and the case, gender and number of the noun described (Case, p. 34).

- **WEAK ENDING** – (the most common adjective endings) — if the noun described is preceded by a **der**-word, such as a definite article, **dies** *(this)*, **jed**- *(each, every)*, **all**- *(all)*, a weak ending suffices.

  The **der**-word itself, not the adjective ending, indicates the case, gender, and number of the noun described: **der gelb**e **Fisch** *(the yellow fish)*, **die blau**en **Autos** *(the blue cars)*.

- **STRONG ENDING**– if the noun described is not preceded by a **der**-word, a strong ending is needed to indicate its case, gender, and number.

  These endings added to the adjective itself often correspond to the endings of articles: **der Fisch** → **gelb**er **Fisch** *(yellow fish)*, **das Auto** → **blau**es **Auto** *(blue car)*.

- **MIXED ENDINGS**– if the noun described is preceded by an **ein**-word There are various types of endings depending on the case of the adjective. Consult your textbook. The Study Tips below will help you memorize them.

Here are the steps to follow to choose the correct ending.

1. Identify the adjective.
2. Identify the noun described.
3. Identify the case, gender, and number of noun above by looking at the word that precedes it
   - if definite article → adjective + weak ending
   - if no article → adjective + strong ending
   - if indefinite article → adjective + mixed ending

Here are some examples.

*Do you know the **new** student (female)?*
1. ADJECTIVE: new
2. NOUN DESCRIBED: ***the** student* → **die** Studentin (feminine singular)
3. DIE: feminine singular accusative → weak ending → **-e**

Kennst du die **neue** Studentin?

*One can find it on the **first** page.*
1. ADJECTIVE: first
2. NOUN DESCRIBED: ***the** page* → **die** Seite (feminine singular)
3. DER: feminine singular dative (prep. **auf** + dative) → weak ending → **-en**

Man kann das auf der **ersten** Seite finden.

*I live in an **old** house.*
1. ADJECTIVE: old
2. NOUN DESCRIBED: ***a** house* → **ein** Haus (neuter singular)
3. EINEM: neuter singular dative (prep. **in** + dative) → mixed ending → **-en**

Ich wohne in einem **alten** Haus.

*Gabi bought a **used** car.*
1. ADJECTIVE: used
2. NOUN DESCRIBED: ***a** car* → **ein** Auto (neuter singular)
3. EIN: neuter singular accusative → mixed ending → **-es**

Gabi hat ein **gebrauchtes** Auto gekauft.

***Blue** skies are on the way.*
1. ADJECTIVE: blue
2. NOUN DESCRIBED: *skies* → Himmel (masculine singular)
3. NO ARTICLE: masculine singular nominative → strong ending → **-er**

Blauer Himmel kommt zum Vorschein.

STUDY TIPS
DESCRIPTIVE ADJECTIVES

Pattern

Learning the patterns of adjective endings is more helpful than trying to learn the endings on their own. As you will see below, some of the forms will be similar to other forms you already know. Compare the pattern of the 3 types of endings of attributive adjectives.

der-words (weak endings)

	Masc.	Fem.	Neut.	Pl.
Nom.	der gelb**e** Fisch	die rot**e** Blume	das blau**e** Auto	die bunt**en** Autos
Acc.	den gelb**en** Fisch	die rot**e** Blume	das blau**e** Auto	die bunt**en** Autos
Dat.	dem gelb**en** Fisch	der rot**en** Blume	dem blau**en** Aut	den bunt**en** Autos
Gen.	des gelb**en** Fisches	der rot**en** Blume	des blau**en** Autos	der bunt**en** Autos

What patterns do you see?

- endings → **-e** or **-en**
- nom. sing. endings → **-e**
- acc. sing. endings: fem. and neut. → **-e;** masc. → **-en**
- dative, genitive, and plural endings → **-en**

No article (strong endings)

	Masc.	Fem.	Neut.	Pl.
Nom.	gelb**er** Fisch	rot**e** Blume	blau**es** Auto	bunt**e** Autos
Acc.	gelb**en** Fisch	rot**e** Blume	blau**es** Auto	bunt**e** Autos
Dat.	gelb**em** Fisch	rot**er** Blume	blau**em** Auto	bunt**en** Autos
Gen.	gelb**es** Fisches	rot**er** Blume	blau**es** Autos	bunt**er** Autos

What pattern do you see?

- endings → same as definite articles (see above and Case, p.34).

ein-words (mixed endings)

	Masc.	Fem.	Neut.	Pl.
Nom.	ein gelb**er** Fisch	eine rot**e** Blume	ein blau**es** Auto	keine bunt**en** Autos
Acc.	einen gelb**en** Fisch	eine rot**e** Blume	ein blau**es** Auto	keine bunt**en** Autos
Dat.	einem gelb**en** Fisch	einer rot**en** Blume	einem blau**en** Auto	keinen bunt**en** Autos
Gen.	eines gelb**en** Fisches	einer rot**en** Blume	eines blau**en** Autos	keiner bunt**en** Autos

What patterns do you see?

- nom. and acc. sing. strong endings → same as definite articles– another way to say this is that ***der***-words show the gender in the nominative and ***ein***-words do not, which requires the adjective to show the gender instead.
- dat., gen., and pl. weak endings → **–en**

Practice

① Create a list of common adjectives.

② Write sentences using those adjectives as attributive adjectives with both **der**-words and **ein**-words to describe masc., fem., neut. sing. and pl. nouns functioning as subjects, indirect, and direct objects.

Subject → nominative case

Der junge Mann geht ins Restaurant.
The young man *goes to the restaurant.*

Ein junger Mann geht ins Restaurant.
A young man *goes to the restaurant.*

Direct object → accusative case

Die Frau sieht **den jungen Mann.**
The woman sees ***the young man.***

Die Frau sieht **einen jungen Mann.**
The woman sees ***a young man.***

Indirect object → dative case

Die Frau gibt **dem jungen Mann** die Karte.
The woman gives ***the young man*** *the menu.*

Die Frau gibt **einem jungen Mann** die Karte.
The woman gives ***a young man*** *the menu.*

Possessor → genitive case

Der Hund **des jungen Mannes** sitzt neben ihm.
The young man's *dog sits beside him.*

Der Hund **eines jungen Mannes** sitzt neben ihm.
A young man's *dog sits beside him.*

REVIEW ACTIVITY

Underline the adjective in the following sentences. Indicate which set of adjective endings you need in German: after der word (AD), after ein-word (AE), no article (NA):

a.	The child plays in front of a red door.	AD	AE	NA
b.	The fresh juice tastes good.	AD	AE	NA
c.	Old shoes are comfortable.	AD	AE	NA
d.	I'll have the large pizza.	AD	AE	NA
e.	That's a friendly face.	AD	AE	NA
f.	No green grass was left on the field in winter.	AD	AE	NA

31 WHAT IS MEANT BY COMPARISON OF ADJECTIVES?

The term **COMPARISON OF ADJECTIVES** is used for descriptive adjectives which compare the degree of the same quality in two or more persons or things (Descriptive adjectives, p. 117).

comparison of adjectives

Hansel is *tall* but Gretel is *taller*.
adjective modifies *Hansel* — adjective modifies *Gretel*

Both nouns, *Hansel* and *Gretel*, have the same quality indicated by the adjective *tall*, and we want to show that Gretel has a greater degree of that quality (i.e., she is *taller* than Hansel).

In English and in German, there are two types of comparison: comparative and superlative.

31.1 COMPARATIVE

The comparative compares a quality of a person or thing with the same quality in another person or thing. The comparison can indicate that one or the other has more, less, or the same amount of that quality.

IN ENGLISH

Let's go over the three degrees of comparison.

The comparative of **GREATER DEGREE** (more) is formed differently depending on the length of the adjective being compared.

- short adjective + *-er* + *than*

  Gretel is tall*er than* Hansel.
  Ingrid is young*er than* her sister.

- *more* + longer adjective + *than*

  Axel is *more* intelligent *than* Franz.
  His car is *more* expensive *than* ours.

The comparative of **LESSER DEGREE** (less) is formed as follows: *not as* + adjective + *as*, or *less* + adjective + *than*.

Hansel is *not as* tall *as* Gretel.
My car is *less* expensive *than* your car.

The comparative of **EQUAL DEGREE** (same) is formed as follows: *as* + adjective + *as*

Axel is *as* tall *as* Franz.
My car is *as* expensive *as* his car.

IN GERMAN

As in English, the comparative has the same three degrees of comparison of adjectives. Unlike English, the structure used does not depend on the length of the adjective.

The comparative of **GREATER DEGREE** is formed by adding **-er** to the stem. Some adjectives, mostly one-syllable words, also add an umlaut to the stem vowels **a, o,** and **u** of the adjective + **-er,** and like in English some change stems irregularly. Unlike English, all German comparatives of greater degrees are compared with endings rather than with the addition of the word **mehr** (more).

The structure and the ending is different for predicate and attributive adjectives (p. 118).

- **PREDICATE ADJECTIVE** – The comparative is the two-word form: adjective + umlaut if necessary + **-er** + **als** *(than)*.

  Ingrid ist jüng**er als** ihr Bruder.
  predicate adjective + umlaut + **-er** + **als**
  *Ingrid is young**er than** her brother.*

  Das Buch ist interessant**er als** der Film.
  predicate adjective + **-er** + **als**
  *The book is **more** interesting **than** the film.*

- **ATTRIBUTIVE ADJECTIVE** – The comparative is the one-word form: adjective + umlaut if necessary + **-er-** + adjective ending, i.e., weak, strong, or mixed.

  Ich kenne das jüng**ere** Mädchen nicht.
  attributive adjective + umlaut + **-er-** + weak ending
  *I don't know the young**er** girl.*

  Das ist ein interessant**erer** Film.
  attributive adjective + **-er-** + mixed ending **-er**
  *That is a **more** interesting film.*

Do not confuse the comparative **-er** ending with the regular **-er** adjective ending.

Regular adjective	**Comparative adjective**
ein **bunter** Garten *a **colorful** garden*	ein bunter**er** Garten *a **more** colorful garden*
ein **kleiner** Hund *a **small** dog*	ein kleiner**er** Hund *a small**er** dog*

The comparative of **LESSER DEGREE** is formed with **nicht so** *(less)* + adjective + **wie** *(than)*.

Tina ist **nicht so gross wie** Franz.
Tina is ***not as tall as*** *Franz.*

Tina ist **nicht so jung wie** Ingrid.
Tina is **not as young as** *Ingrid.*

The comparative of **EQUAL DEGREE** is formed with **so** *(as)* + adjective + **wie** *(as)*.

Axel ist **so gross wie** Anja.
Axel is ***as tall as*** *Anja.*

Mein Auto ist **so teuer wie** sein Auto.
My car is ***as expensive as*** *his car.*

31.2 SUPERLATIVE

The superlative form is used to stress the highest or lowest degrees of a quality.

IN ENGLISH

Let's go over the two degrees of the superlative.

The superlative of **HIGHEST DEGREE** is formed differently depending on the length of the adjective.

- *the* + short adjective + *-est*

  Ingrid is *the* calm*est* in the family.
  My car is *the* saf*est* on the market.

- *the most* + long adjective

  That argument was *the most* convincing.
  This book is *the most* interesting of all.

The superlative of **LOWEST DEGREE** is formed as follows: *the least* + adjective.

Hans is *the least* active.
Her car is *the least* expensive of all.

IN GERMAN

As in English, there are two degrees of the superlative.

The superlative of **HIGHEST DEGREE** is formed by adding **-est** to the stem. Some adjectives, mostly one-syllable words, also add an umlaut to the stem vowels **a, o,** and **u** of the adjective + **-est,** and like in English some change stems irregularly. Unlike English, all German superlatives of the highest degree are formed with ending changes rather than the addition of the word **meist** *(most).*

The structure and the ending of the superlative form is different for predicate (the form listed in the dictionary) and attributive adjectives.

- **PREDICATE ADJECTIVE** – The superlative is the two word form: **am** + adjective + umlaut if necessary + (**-st-** or **-est-**) + **-en.**

  Dieses Buch ist **am** **ä**lt**esten.**
  *This book is **the** old**est**.*

  Inge ist **am** klein**sten.**
  *Inge is **the** small**est**.*

- **ATTRIBUTIVE ADJECTIVE** – The superlative is the two-word form: definite article + adjective + umlaut if necessary + **(-st-** or **-est)** + weak adjective ending.

  Hier ist **das ä**lt**este** Buch.
  *Here is **the** old**est** book.*

  Inge ist **das** klein**ste** Mädchen in der Schule.
  *Inge is **the** small**est** girl in the school.*

The superlative of **LOWEST DEGREE** is a three-word form: **am wenigsten** + adjective.

Hans ist **am wenigsten** flexibel.
*Hans is **the least** flexible.*

Ihr Auto ist **am wenigsten** teuer.
*Her car is **the least** expensive.*

CAREFUL – In English and in German there are several adjectives that form the comparative and the superlative in irregular ways.

good	gut	*much*	viel
better	besser	*more*	mehr
best	am besten	*most*	am meisten

You will find a list of irregular comparative and superlative forms in your German textbook that you will have to memorize.

STUDY TIPS

COMPARATIVE OF ADJECTIVES

Flashcards

As you learn new adjectives, it is useful to both write and practice the attributive and well as the predicate forms of comparison. The dictionary form of the superlative **(am -sten)** is only used as the predicate. You can indicate the attributive form as follows: **groß, größer, am größten (größt-)** the hyphen indicates that an ending is necessary.

REVIEW ACTIVITY

Using the words given, write sentences with comparative adjectives. The various degrees of comparison are indicated as follows:

++	superlative
+	greater degree
=	equal degree
–	lesser degree

a. The teacher is / (+) old / the students.

____

b. This student is / (=) intelligent / that one.

____

c. Kathy is / (–) tall / Molly.

____

d. This movie is / (++) good / this season.

____

e. Today is / (++) hot / day on record.

____

f. That is /(+) interesting/ than what I heard about it yesterday!

____

WHAT IS THE POSSESSIVE? 32

The **POSSESSIVE** is the form used to show that one noun *possesses* or owns another noun, or that two nouns have various types of relationship, for example, a spatial relationship or a part of a whole.

> The teacher's German book is on her desk.
> (teacher's: noun possessor; book: noun possessed)
>
> The side of the house was painted blue.
> (side: noun possessed; house: noun possessor)

32.1 IN ENGLISH

There are two constructions to show possession.

APOSTROPHE — In this construction the possessor comes before the noun possessed.

- a singular possessor adds an apostrophe + "s"

  Gabi's mother
  the professor's book
  (professor's: singular possessor)

- a plural possessor ending with "s" adds an apostrophe after the "s"

  the girls' father
  the boys' school
  (boys': plural possessor)

- a plural possessor not ending with "s" adds an apostrophe + "s"

  the children's playground
  the women's role
  (women's: plural possessor)

THE WORD "OF" — In this construction the noun possessed comes before the possessor.

- a singular or plural possessor is preceded by "*of the*" or "*of a*"

  the book *of the* professor
  the branches *of a* tree
  (professor, tree: singular possessor)

  the teacher *of the* students
  (students: plural possessor)

- a proper noun possessor is preceded by *of*

  the poetry *of* Goethe
  (Goethe: proper noun possessor)

32.2 IN GERMAN

There are also two ways to show possession: the genitive case is used in writing and in formal language and **von** + the dative case is used in spoken German (Case, p. 32).

GENITIVE CASE — When the genitive case of a noun is used to show possession, the order in which the noun possessor and the noun possessed appear is different depending on whether the noun possessor is a proper or a common noun.

- **PROPER NOUN POSSESSOR** – This German structure parallels the English structure that uses the apostrophe to show possession. Just as in English, the noun possessor, in this case a proper noun, comes before the noun possessed.

  Inges Mutter
  Inge's *mother*
  possessor possessed

  In German the only time that an apostrophe is used for the genitive is when a proper noun ends in -s or -z.

  Kiwus' Gedichte
  Kiwus's *poems*
  possessor possessed

- **COMMON NOUN POSSESSOR** – This German structure parallels the English structure that uses *of*. Just as in English, the noun possessor, in this case a common noun, generally follows the noun possessed. Note that the genitive case does not require a preposition.

  Most masculine and neuter singular nouns of one syllable → add **-es.** Masculine and neuter singular nouns of more than one syllable → add **-s.** The accompanying articles also end in **-s.**

  der Sportler **des** Jahr**es**
  possessed — *athlete*
  genitive definite article
  possessor — *year* — neuter singular, one syllable **Jahr**

  the athlete ***of the*** *year*
  *the year****'s*** *(best) athlete*

  Feminine singular and plural nouns → add **-er** to the preceding article or adjectives. The noun itself has no special ending.

der Mantel der Frau

possessed — *coat* | genitive definite article | possessor — *woman* — *feminine*

*the coat **of the** woman*
*the woman**'s** coat*

Your German textbook will explain the genitive in greater detail and will point out the few irregularities.

- **VON + DATIVE** – When the construction **von** + dative case is used to show possession, the same construction is used for proper and common noun possessor. The order in which the noun possessor and the noun possessed appear corresponds to the construction *of* + noun possessor in English.

  der Vater **von den** Mädchen
  (von + dative)

  *the father **of the** girls*

  die Mutter **von** Inge
  *the mother **of** Inge*

CAREFUL – A common error with the possessive occurs when translating the phrase "at the house of." In German, this phrase is constructed with the preposition **bei** *(at* meaning *at the house of)* followed by a noun or pronoun referring to a person or persons in the dative case.

at *my friend's* house — **bei** meinem Freund.
(**bei**: preposition, *at the house of*; meinem Freund: dative, *my friend*)

Your textbook or a dictionary will help you identify other instances where each language treats the possessive differently.

REVIEW ACTIVITY

The following are possessive constructions using the apostrophe.

I. Write the alternate English structure using "*of*".
II. Underline the possessor in your new construction.

a. the cars' motor ______________________
b. the year's end ______________________
c. Bachmann's works ______________________
d. the street's name ______________________
e. Berlin's museums ______________________
f. the book's introduction ______________________

WHAT IS A POSSESSIVE ADJECTIVE? 33

A **POSSESSIVE ADJECTIVE** is a word that describes a noun by showing who possesses that noun.

> Whose house is that? It's my house.
> describes the noun *house* and shows who possesses it, *I do*

33.1 IN ENGLISH

Like subject pronouns, possessive adjectives are identified according to the person they represent (Personal pronouns, p. 40).

Singular possessor

1st person		my
2nd person		your
3rd person	Masculine	his
	Feminine	her
	Neuter	its

Plural possessor

1st person	our
2nd person	your
3rd person	their

A possessive adjective only identifies the possessor. The same form is used regardless of the object possessed.

> Is that Axel's house? Yes, it is *his* house.
> Is that Ingrid's house? Yes, it is *her* house.
> Although the object possessed is the same *(house)*, different possessive adjectives *(his* and *her)* are used because the possessors are different *(Axel* and *Ingrid)*.

> Is that Axel's house? Yes, it is *his* house.
> Are those Axel's keys? Yes, they are *his* keys.
> Although the objects possessed are different *(house* and *keys)*, the same possessive adjective *(his)* is used because the possessor is the same *(Axel)*.

33.2 IN GERMAN

Like English, a German possessive adjective changes to identify the possessor. Unlike English, however, and like all German adjectives, it also agrees in case, gender, and number with the noun possessed.

33.2

To choose the correct form of the possessive adjective follow these steps:

1. Find the possessor.

Singular possessor

1st person		mein-	*my*
2nd person	Familiar	dein-	*your*
	Formal	Ihr-	*your*
3rd person	Masculine	sein-	*his*
	Feminine	ihr-	*her*
	Neuter	sein-	*its*

Plural possessor

1st person		unser-	*our*
2nd person	Familiar	euer-	*your*
	Formal	Ihr-	*your*
3rd person		ihr-	*their*

2. Identify and analyze the noun possessed.
   - What is its case?
   - What is its gender?
   - What is its number?

3. Provide the ending that corresponds to the case, gender, and number of the noun possessed. These endings are the same as those for the indefinite articles **(ein, eine, ein)** (Articles, p. 25; Case, p. 35). Because they follow the same pattern as indefinite articles, your textbook may refer to possessive adjectives as "**ein-**words."

Let us apply the above steps to examples.

He always forgets ***his*** *books.*
1. POSSESSOR: *his* → **sein-**
2. NOUN POSSESSED: *books*
   CASE: **vergessen** *(to forget)* takes a direct object → accusative
   GENDER: **das Buch** *(book)* → neuter
   NUMBER: *books* → plural
3. ENDING: accusative neuter plural → **-e**

Er vergißt immer **seine** Bücher.

She gives ***her*** *brother the telephone number.*
1. POSSESSOR: *her* → **ihr-**
2. NOUN POSSESSED: *brother*
   CASE: indirect object of **geben** *(to give)* → dative
   (She gives the number *to whom?* Her brother.)
   GENDER: **der Bruder** *(brother)* → *masculine*
   NUMBER: *brother* → singular
3. ENDING: dative masculine singular → **-em**

Sie gibt **ihrem** Bruder die Telefonnummer.

CAREFUL – Remember that **ihr**- with an ending and followed by a noun is a possessive adjective that can mean *her* or *their* depending on the possessor. If **ihr** has no ending and is not in front of a noun, it is a pronoun and it can mean either *you* (nominative, familiar plural) or *her* (dative singular). If **Ihr** is capitalized anywhere other than the first word in a sentence, it is the formal second person (*your* in the singular or plural). If it is capitalized as the first word in a sentence, you will need to rely on other contextual information to deterrmine the meaning.

STUDY TIPS

POSSESSIVE ADJECTIVES

Flashcards

Make a flashcard for each possessive pronoun. On the German side, write the possessive adjective with a dash following it to indicate that an ending it needed. On the English side, write the translation.

unser-	*our*
ihr-	*her, their*

Pattern

Review the case endings for indefinite articles p. 35. These are the endings for possessive adjectives.

REVIEW ACTIVITY

Underline the possessive adjective in the following sentences. Circle the noun possessed.

a. The students took their exams home.

b. Susan put on her coat and her scarf.

c. Tom put his comb in his pocket.

d. My backpack must be somewhere in my room.

34 WHAT IS A POSSESSIVE PRONOUN?

A **POSSESSIVE PRONOUN** is a word that replaces a noun and indicates the possessor of that noun. The word *possessive* comes from *possess*, to own.

> Whose house is that? It's mine.
>
> replaces the noun *house*, the object possessed, and shows who possesses it, *I do.*

34.1 IN ENGLISH

Like subject pronouns, possessive pronouns are identified according to the person they represent (Personal pronouns, p. 40).

Singular possessor

1st person		mine
2nd person		yours
3rd person	Masculine	his
	Feminine	hers
	Neuter	its

Plural possessor

1st person	ours
2nd person	yours
3rd person	theirs

A possessive pronoun only identifies the possessor. The same form is used regardless of the object possessed.

> My car is red; what color is Axel's? His is blue.
>
> 3rd pers. masc. sing.
>
> Axel's car is blue. What color is yours? Mine is white.
>
> 1st pers. sing.
>
> Although the object possessed is the same *(car)*, different possessive pronouns *(his* and *mine)* are used because the possessors are different *(Axel* and *I)*.
>
> Is that Axel's house? Yes, it is *his*.
> Are those Axel's keys? Yes, they are *his*.
>
> Although the objects possessed are different *(house* and *keys)*, the same possessive pronoun *(his)* is used because the possessor is the same *(Axel)*.

34.2 IN GERMAN

Like English, a German possessive pronoun refers to the possessor. Unlike English, however, and like all German pronouns, it also agrees in gender and number with the antecedent, that is, with the person or object possessed. In addition, the appropriate case ending is added to the possessive pronoun to reflect its function in the sentence.

Let us look at the German possessive pronouns to which the case endings are added.

Singular possessor			
1st person		mein-	*mine*
2nd person	Informal	dein-	*yours*
	Formal	Ihr-	*yours*
3rd person	Masculine	sein-	*his*
	Feminine	ihr-	*her*
	Neuter	sein-	*its*
Plural possessor			
1st person		unser-	*ours*
2nd person	Informal	euer-	*yours*
	Formal	Ihr-	*yours*
3rd person		ihr-	*theirs*

The case endings of possessive pronouns are essentially the same as those of the possessive adjectives (Possessive adjectives, p. 131), with the exception of the masculine and neuter nominative singular and the neuter accusative singular, which all share the ending -s. Your textbook will explain how to recognize possessive pronouns.

REVIEW ACTIVITY

Circle the possessive pronouns in the following sentences.

a. I have my book; do you have yours?

b. Did your parents come? Ours stayed home.

c. Whose report was the best? Hers was.

d. Did somebody forget this jacket? Yes, it's his.

e. Let me see those keys: I bet they're mine.

35 WHAT IS AN INTERROGATIVE ADJECTIVE?

An **INTERROGATIVE ADJECTIVE** is a word that asks for information about a noun.

> Which book do you want?
> asks information about the noun *book*

35.1 IN ENGLISH

The words *which* and *what* are called interrogative adjectives when they come in front of a noun and are used to ask a question about that noun. Sometimes the noun is not stated when it is obvious from the context.

> *Which* instructor is teaching the course?
> *What* courses are you taking?
> We are watching two films. *Which* is longer?
> which [film]

35.2 IN GERMAN

The stem of the interrogative adjective is **welch-** *(which, what)*. Like all adjectives in German, the ending changes to agree in case, gender, and number with the noun modified. To choose the correct ending:

1. Identify and analyze the noun modified.
   - What is its case?
   - What is its gender and number?
2. Provide the ending that corresponds to the case, gender, and number of the noun modified. These endings are the same as those for the definite articles **der, die, das** (Articles, p. 45). Because they follow the same pattern as definite articles, except in the neuter singular nominative and accusative where the ending **-es** replaces **-as,** your textbook may refer to interrogative adjectives as "**der**-words."

Let us apply the above steps to examples.

> ***Which** lamp is cheaper?*
> 1. NOUN MODIFIED: lamp
>   CASE: subject of to be **(sein)** → nominative
>   GENDER & NUMBER: **die Lampe** *(lamp)*→ feminine singular
> 2. ENDING: nominative feminine singular → **-e**
>
> **Welche** Lampe ist billiger?

> ***Which** (what) dress do you want to wear?*
> 1. NOUN MODIFIED: dress
>   CASE: direct object of *to wear* (**tragen**) → accusative
>   GENDER & NUMBER: **das Kleid** *(dress)* → neuter singular
> 2. ENDING: accusative neuter singular → **-es**
>
> **Welches** Kleid willst du tragen?

Which *man do we give our tickets to?*

1. NOUN MODIFIED: man
   CASE: indirect object of *to give* (**geben**) → dative
   GENDER & NUMBER: **der Mann** *(man)* → masculine singular
2. ENDING: dative masculine singular → **-em**

Welchem Mann geben wir unsere Karten?

The interrogative adjective agrees in case, gender and number with the noun it modifies even if the noun is not stated.

Wir schauen uns zwei Filme an. → **Welcher** ist länger? (welcher Film)

1. NOUN MODIFIED: film
   CASE: subject of *to be* (**sein**) → nominative
   GENDER & NUMBER: **der Film** *(film)* → masculine singular
2. ENDING: nominative masculine singular → **-er**

We are watching two films. → ***Which*** *is longer? (which film)*

INTERROGATIVE ADJECTIVE AS OBJECT OF A PREPOSITION

When expressing an English question with an interrogative Adjective in German, be sure to restructure any dangling preposition (p. 76). Begin the question with the preposition, followed by the interrogative adjective in the case required by that preposition.

Which *street does he live* ***on?*** *→* ***On which*** *street does he live?*

1. NOUN MODIFIED: street
   CASE: object of preposition *on* (**in**) → dative
   GENDER & NUMBER: **die Straße** *(street)* → feminine singular
2. ENDING: dative feminine singular → **-er**

In welcher Straße wohnt er?

What *film are you talking* ***about?*** *→* ***About what*** *film are you talking?*

1. NOUN MODIFIED: film
   CASE: object of preposition *about* (**über**) → accusative
   GENDER & NUMBER: **der Film** *(film)* → masculine singular
2. ENDING: accusative masculine singular → **-en**

Über welchen Film sprecht ihr?

CAREFUL – The word *what* is not always an interrogative adjective. It can also be an interrogative pronoun. When it is a pronoun, *what* is not followed by a noun (p. 130).

What *is on the table?*
interrogative pronoun
Was ist auf dem Tisch?

It is important that you distinguish interrogative adjectives from interrogative pronouns because, in German, different words are used, and they follow different rules.

REVIEW ACTIVITY

I. Underline the interrogative adjective in the following sentences. Circle the noun about which the question is being asked.

a. What newspaper do you read?
b. Which record did you buy?
c. Do you know what homework is due?
d. Which hotel are you staying at?
e. Which game did you see?
f. What car do they drive?

II. Rewrite these questions in English to eliminate the dangling prepositions.

a. Which topic did you write about?

____

b. Which people did you talk to?

____

WHAT IS AN INTERROGATIVE PRONOUN? 36

An **INTERROGATIVE PRONOUN** is a word that replaces a noun and introduces a question. The word *interrogative* comes from *interrogate,* to question.

> Who is coming for dinner?
> question referring to a person
>
> What did you eat for dinner?
> question referring to a thing

In both English and German, a different interrogative pronoun is used depending on whether it refers to a "person" (human beings and live animals) or a "thing" (objects and ideas). In addition, the form of the interrogative pronoun often changes according to its function in the sentence: subject, direct object, indirect object, or object of a preposition. We shall look at each type separately.

36.1 REFERRING TO A PERSON

IN ENGLISH

There are three interrogative pronouns referring to persons.

Who is used for the subject of the sentence (Subject, p. 44).

> Who lives here?
> subject
>
> Who told you about that?
> subject

Whom is used for the direct object, indirect object (p. 63), and object of a preposition (p. 80).

> Whom do you know here?
> direct object
>
> (To) whom did you write a note?
> indirect object
>
> From whom did you get the book?
> object of preposition *from*

In spoken English *who* is often used instead of *whom* for direct and indirect objects, and for objects of a preposition. It is only by using the formal structure of questions and restructuring dangling prepositions (p. 76) that you will be able to establish the function of the interrogative pronoun: is it a subject or an object of some kind?

Who do you know here?
  Verb: know
  Subject: Who knows? *You* → subject
  Object: You know who(m)? *Who* → object
Whom do you know here?

Who did you speak to?
  Dangling Preposition: to
  Object: who → whom → object of preposition *to*
To whom did you speak?

Whose, the possessive form, is used to ask about possession or ownership.

There's a pencil on the floor? Whose is it?
(Whose = possessive)

They are nice cars. Whose are they?
(Whose = possessive)

IN GERMAN

There are four forms of interrogative pronouns depending on the case required, that is, one form for each case. Number and gender do not affect interrogative pronouns.

To select the proper form of the interrogative pronoun you will have to determine its function in the German sentence by asking the following five questions:

1. Is it the subject of the question?
2. Is it the direct object of the German verb? Does that verb take an accusative or dative direct object?
3. Is it the indirect object of the German verb?
4. Is it the object of a preposition? If so, does that German preposition take the accusative or dative, or genitive?
5. Is it the possessive pronoun *whose?*

Subject — *who?* → (nom.) **wer?** — can refer to both singular and plural subjects.

***Who** is in the room? The teacher is in the room.*
Wer ist in dem Zimmer? Die Lehrerin ist in dem Zimmer.

***Who** is coming this evening? Hans and Anja are coming.*
Wer kommt heute abend? Hans und Anja kommen.

As in English, the verb that goes with *who* is singular when it is used generally or the answer is unknown. However, it may be plural when addressing specific people.

***Who** are they?*
Wer sind sie?

Object — *whom?* → (acc.) **wen?** or (dat.) **wem?** — depending on the case required in German. Be sure to restructure dangling prepositions.

> ***Who(m)*** *do you see?*
> **Wen** sehen Sie?
> direct object → accusative

> ***Who(m)*** *are they helping?*
> **Wem** helfen sie?
> verb **helfen** *(to help)* → dative direct object

> ***Who*** *is he speaking* ***about?*** → ***About whom*** *is he speaking?*
> **Über wen** spricht er?
> preposition **über** *(about)* → accusative object of a preposition

> ***Who*** *did he tell the story* ***to?*** → ***To whom*** *did he tell the story?*
> **Wem** hat er die Geschichte erzählt?
> indirect object → dative

> ***Who*** *are you coming* ***with?*** → ***With whom*** *are you coming?*
> **Mit wem** kommst du?
> preposition **mit** *(with)* → dative object of a preposition

Possessive — *whose?* → (gen.) **wessen?** — can refer to both singular and plural possessors.

> ***Whose*** *car is that?*
> **Wessen** Auto ist das?
> possessor → genitive

36.2 REFERRING TO A THING

IN ENGLISH

There is one interrogative pronoun referring to things or ideas.

What is used for subject, direct object, indirect object, and the object of a preposition.

> *What* happened?
> subject

> *What* do you want?
> direct object

> *What* is the movie about?
> object of preposition *about*

CAREFUL – The word *what* is not always an interrogative pronoun. It can also be an interrogative adjective (p. 136).

IN GERMAN

As in English, there is only one interrogative pronoun referring to things or ideas.

Was *(what)* is used as a subject or a direct object.

> **Was** ist in diesem Paket?
> ***What*** *is in this package?*
>
> **Was** machst du?
> ***What*** *are you doing?*

A construction called the **WO-COMPOUND** is used when the interrogative pronoun *what* is the object of some prepositions. It is formed by adding the prefix **wo-** (**wor-** if the preposition begins with a vowel) to the preposition.

Here are two examples.

> ***What*** *are you talking* ***about?***
> **Wovon** redet ihr?
> **wo-** + **von** *(about)*
>
> ***What*** *is he waiting* ***for?***
> **Worauf** wartet er?
> **wor-** + **auf** *(for)*

Your German textbook will discuss this construction and its use in greater detail.

36.3 SUMMARY

Here is a chart you can use as reference.

Interrogative Pronoun		
Referring to persons		
Nominative	wer	*who*
Accusative	wen	*whom*
Dative	wem	*whom*
Genitive	wessen	*whose*
Referring to things	was	*what*
	wo(r)- + prep.	

STUDY TIPS
INTERROGATIVE PRONOUNS

Pattern

Compare the interrogative pronouns with the masculine forms of other parts of speech, such as personal pronouns and definite articles.

	Interrogative pronoun	**Personal article**	**Definite pronoun**
Nominative	wer	er	der
Accusative	wen	ihn	den
Dative	wem	ihm	dem
Genitive	wessen		des

What similarities do you see?

-r, -n-, -m, -s mark the case of these pronouns and masculine articles.

- nominative forms end in –**r**
- accusative forms end in –**n**
- dative forms end in –**m**
- genitive forms have an –**s**

36.3

REVIEW ACTIVITY

Underline the interrogative pronouns in the following sentences, restructuring where appropriate.

i. Indicate the type of the antecedent: Person or Thing
ii. Indicate the function of the antecedent: subject **(S)**, direct object **(DO)**, indirect object **(ID)**, or object of a preposition **(OP)**.
iii. Write the appropriate German interrogative pronoun using the information given.

a. Who read the book?

Type of antecedent:	Person	Thing		
Function:	S	DO	IO	OP

________________ hat das Buch gelesen?

b. What did she say?

Type of antecedent:	Person	Thing		
Function:	S	DO	IO	OP

________________ hat sie gesagt?

c. Whose car is that?

Type of antecedent:	Person	Thing		
Function:	S	DO	IO	OP

________________ Auto ist das?

d. Who are we waiting for?

Type of antecedent:	Person	Thing		
Function:	S	DO	IO	OP

(to wait for = ***warten auf*** + accusative)

Auf ________________ warten wir?

WHAT IS A DEMONSTRATIVE ADJECTIVE? 37

A **DEMONSTRATIVE ADJECTIVE** is a word used to refer to a specific noun.

> *This* book is interesting.
> refers to a specific *book* (noun)

37.1 IN ENGLISH

The demonstrative adjectives are *this* and *that* in the singular and *these* and *those* in the plural. They are rare examples of English adjectives agreeing in number with the noun they modify: *this* changes to *these* and *that* changes to *those* when they modify a plural noun (p. 16).

Singular	**Plural**
this cat	*these* cats
that man	*those* men

This and *these* refer to persons or objects near the speaker, and *that* and *those* refer to persons or objects away from the speaker.

37.2 IN GERMAN

The stems of the demonstrative adjectives are **dies-** *(this)*, **jen-** *(that)*, and **jed-** *(every)*. Like all adjectives in German, the ending changes to agree in case, gender, and number with the noun modified. To choose the correct ending:

1. Identify and analyze the noun modified.
   - What is its case?
   - What is its gender?
   - What is its number?
2. Provide the ending that corresponds to the case, gender, and number of the noun modified. These endings are the same as those for the definite articles (Articles, p. 25; Case, p. 32). Because they follow the same pattern as definite articles, except in the neuter singular nominative and accusative where the ending **-es** replaces **-as,** your textbook may refer to the demonstrative adjectives as "**der**-words."

Let us apply the above steps to some examples.

> ***This** room is large.*
> 1. NOUN MODIFIED: room
>   CASE: subject of **sein** *(to be)* → nominative
>   GENDER & NUMBER: **das Zimmer** *(room)* → neuter singular
> 2. ENDING: nominative neuter singular ending → **-es**
>
> **Dieses** Zimmer ist gross.

Show **every** *person the house.*

1. NOUN MODIFIED: person
   CASE: indirect object of **zeigen** *(to show)* → dative
   GENDER & NUMBER: **die Person** *(person)* → feminine singular
2. ENDING: dative feminine singular ending → **-er**

Zeig **jeder** Person das Haus.

Have you seen ***these*** *men?*

1. NOUN MODIFIED: men
   CASE: direct object of **sehen** *(to see)* → accusative
   GENDER: **der Mann** *(man)* → masculine plural
   NUMBER: **die Männer** *(men)* → plural
2. ENDING: accusative masculine plural ending → **-e**

Haben Sie **diese** Männer gesehen?

REVIEW ACTIVITY

Circle the demonstrative adjective in the sentences below.
Draw an arrow from the demonstrative adjective to the noun it modifies.

a. Did you see every room?

b. I prefer this house.

c. All houses are expensive.

d. These windows are nice.

e. Those closets are large.

WHAT IS A DEMONSTRATIVE PRONOUN? 38

A **DEMONSTRATIVE PRONOUN** is a word that stands for a noun as if pointing to it. The word *demonstrative* comes from *demonstrate,* to show. It refers to a previously expressed noun, called the **ANTECEDENT**, or to an entire statement.

> Choose a book. *This one* is in English. *These* are in German.
> book → antecedent; *This one* → points to a book; *These* → points to other books

38.1 IN ENGLISH

The most common demonstrative pronouns are *this (one)* and *that (one)* to refer to one person or thing, and *these* and *those* to refer to more than one person or thing.

> I have two groups of students. *These* speak German ; *those* do not.
> students → antecedent; *These* → plural, close to speaker; *those* → plural, further away

This (one), these refer to something or someone near the speaker, and *that (one), those* refer to things or persons further away from the speaker.

38.2 IN GERMAN

The most common demonstrative pronouns are the following:

dieser	*this, these*
jener	*that, those*

The demonstrative pronoun agrees in gender with its antecedent, its number depends on whether it refers to one thing *(this one, that one)* or to more than one person or object *(these, those),* and its case depends on its function in the sentence.

To choose the correct form, follow these steps:

1. Determine the location of the item pointed out in relation to the speaker or the person spoken to.
2. Find the antecedent.
3. Determine the gender of the antecedent.
4. Determine the number of the antecedent: *this one, that one* → singular; *these, those* → plural.
5. Based on steps 2, 3, and 4 choose the German equivalent.
6. Add the case endings required by the function of the demonstrative pronoun.
7. Make a selection based on the steps 3-6 above.

38.2

Look at the following examples.

Which train should we take? Let's take ***this one.***

1. Relationship: this → near the speaker
2. Antecedent: train (**Zug**)
3. Gender: **der Zug** → masculine
4. Number: this one → singular
5. German Word: **dies-**
6. Case: direct object → accusative
7. Selection: **dies-** + masc. sing, acc. → **–en**

Welchen Zug sollen wir nehmen? Nehmen wir **diesen.**

Do you know this woman? No, but I know ***that one.***

1. Relationship: that → further away from speaker
2. Antecedent: woman (**Frau**)
3. Gender: **die Frau** → feminine
4. Number: that one → singular
5. German Word: **jen-**
6. Case: direct object → accusative
7. Selection: **jen-** + fem. sing. acc. → **-e**

Kennst du diese Frau? Nein, aber ich kenne **jene.**

WHAT IS A SENTENCE? 39

A **SENTENCE** is a group of words that work together as a complete meaningful unit. In written form, a sentence begins with a capital letter and ends with a period, a question mark, or an exclamation point. Typically a sentence consists of at least a subject (p. 45) and a verb (p. 29).

> The girls ran.
> subject verb
>
> They were eating.
> subject verb

Depending on the verb, a sentence may also have direct and indirect objects (Chap 63).

> The boy threw the ball.
> subject verb direct object
>
> Maria threw her brother the ball.
> subject verb indirect object direct object

In addition, a sentence may include other words giving additional information about the subject or the verb; these words are called **MODIFIERS.** There are various kinds of modifiers:

- adjective (p. 117)

  I saw a *great* movie.
  adjective

- adverb (p. 165)

  Yesterday I saw a great movie.
  adverb

- prepositional phrase; that is, a group of words that begins with a preposition (p. 74)

  Yesterday *after work* I saw a great movie.
  prepositional phrase

- participial phrase; that is, a group of words that begins with a participle (p. 106).

  Attracted by the reviews, I saw a great movie yesterday.
  participial phrase modifying *I*

- infinitive phrase; that is, a clause that begins with an infinitive (Verbs, p. 29).

  To entertain myself, I saw a movie.
  infinitive phrase

It is important for you to learn to recognize the different types of sentences, clauses, modifiers, and phrases, since in German they affect the order in which words appear in a sentence.

39.2

39.1 SIMPLE SENTENCES

A **SIMPLE SENTENCE** is a sentence consisting of only one **CLAUSE**, namely, a group of words including a subject and a conjugated verb.

IN ENGLISH

There is no set position for the verb in an English sentence or clause, but the subject almost always comes before the verb.

> We are going to the concert.
> subject verb

A modifier can also come before the subject.

> *Today* we are going to a concert.
> adverb

> *After the party* we are going to a concert.
> prepositional phrase

IN GERMAN

In a simple sentence the conjugated verb always stands in second position. This does not mean that the verb is always the second word in the sentence, because some groups of words, such as prepositional phrases, count as one position.

> Wir **essen** in einem Restaurant.
> *we **are eating** in a restaurant*
> subject verb
> 1 2
> We **are eating** in a restaurant.

> Heute **essen** wir in einem Restaurant.
> *today **are eating** we in a restaurant*
> adverb verb subject
> 1 2
> *Today we **are eating** in a restaurant.*

> Vor der Party **essen** wir in einem Restaurant.
> *before the party **are eating** we in a restaurant*
> prep. phrase verb subject
> 1 2
> *Before the party we **are eating** in a restaurant.*

As you can see, only in the first example it is possible to put the subject before the verb. In the other two sentences where there is a modifier in the first position, the subject must follow the verb so that the verb can be in the second position.

39.2 COMPOUND SENTENCES

A **COMPOUND SENTENCE** consists of two main clauses, each with a subject and a conjugated verb, joined by a coordinating conjunction (Conjunctions, p. 155). In each clause, the word order is the same as in a simple sentence.

As in a simple sentence, the position of the verb in each clause may vary, though the subject usually comes before the verb. In the examples below, each clause is underlined.

The sky is grey, *but* it is not raining.
coordinating conjunction

Every evening John plays the piano *and* his sister sings.
coordinating conjunction

It is important that you know how to recognize a compound sentence because the verb must be in the second position of each clause. The coordinating conjunction is just a link between the two simple sentences and does not count as the first position.

Der	Himmel	**ist** grau,	aber	es	**regnet** nicht.
	1	2	conj.	1	2
the	*sky*	***is** grey,*	*but*	*it*	***is raining** not*

*The sky **is** grey, but it **is** not **raining.***

Jeden Abend	**spielt** Max Klavier	und	seine Schwester	**singt.**
1	2	conj.	1	2
every evening	***plays** Max the piano*	*and*	*his sister*	***sings***

*Every evening Max **plays** the piano and his sister **sings.***

39.3 COMPLEX SENTENCES

A **COMPLEX SENTENCE** is a sentence consisting of a main clause and one or more dependent clauses. In the examples below the main clause is underlined; the remainder of the sentence is the dependent clause.

The **MAIN CLAUSE**, also called an **INDEPENDENT CLAUSE**, is a clause that could stand alone as a complete sentence.

The **DEPENDENT CLAUSE**, also called a **SUBORDINATE CLAUSE**, cannot stand alone as a complete sentence because it depends on the main clause for its full meaning.

Before I eat, I always wash my hands.

It makes sense to say "I always wash my hands" without the first clause in the sentence; therefore, it is the main clause. It does not make sense to say, "before I eat" unless we add a main clause; therefore, it is the dependent clause.

IN ENGLISH

Distinguishing a main clause from a dependent clause helps you to write complete sentences and to avoid sentence fragments.

IN GERMAN

It is important for you to learn to distinguish between a main clause and a dependent clause in German, because each type of clause has its own word order rules.

MAIN CLAUSE — the word order depends on whether the main clause is at the beginning of the sentence or at the end.

- at the beginning of the sentence — the verb of the main clause remains in the same position as in the simple sentence; that is, in the second position.

  Ich **wasche** mir immer die Hände, bevor ich esse.
  1 2
  I ***wash*** *myself always the hands before I eat*
  I always ***wash*** *my hands before I eat.*

- at the end of the sentence — the verb of the main clause comes right after the dependent clause that functions as a single unit of meaning and counts as the first position.

  Bevor ich esse, **wasche** ich mir immer die Hände.
  1 2
  before I eat, ***wash*** *I myself always the hands*
  Before I eat, I always ***wash*** *my hands.*

DEPENDENT CLAUSES — the conjugated verb always stands at the end of the dependent clause, regardless if it comes before or after the main clause.

Ich wasche mir die Hände, weil sie schmutzig **sind.**
I wash myself the hands because they dirty ***are***
I wash my hands, because they ***are*** *dirty.*

Weil sie schmutzig **sind,** wasche ich mir die Hände.
because they dirty ***are*** *wash I myself the hands*
Because they ***are*** *dirty, I wash my hands.*

When there is more than one verb in a clause, the conjugated verb is placed at the very end of the dependent clause, after other unconjugated verbs.

> Wir sind in die Stadt gefahren, nachdem wir die Haushaltsarbeiten erledigt **hatten.**
> we are into the city drove after we the chores finished **had**
> *We drove into the city, after we **had** finished the chores.*

Your German textbook will explain this structure in more detail.

STUDY TIPS
SENTENCES

When you practice vocabulary and/or grammar by writing sentences, try to challenge yourself to use multiple clauses linked by conjunctions (p. 161). This will allow you to practice the relevant forms and at the same time practice word order and composing longer thoughts in German.

For example, if you want to practice using the word ***vergessen*** (to forget) in different tenses, you might write

> ***Er vergaß das.***
> He forgot that.

but the following examples would allow you to extend your practice to longer sentences and more complex ideas:

> ***Nachdem er das vergessen hatte, musste er es wieder lernen.***
> After he had forgotten that, he had to learn it again.

> ***Er vergaß, dass er morgen keinen Unterricht hat.***
> He forgot that he doesn't have class tomorrow.

REVIEW ACTIVITY

I. Underline the phrases in these sentences. Identify whether the phrase is a prepositional phrase (PRP), participial phrase (PP), or an infinitive phrase (IP).

a. It is important to do your best.	PRP	PP	IP
b. Before the play we ate out.	PRP	PP	IP
c. Chris remembered the appointment at the last minute.	PRP	PP	IP
d. They wanted to start early.	PRP	PP	IP
e. Jane spent an hour organizing her room.	PRP	PP	IP
f. Listening to loud music gave her a headache.	PRP	PP	IP

II. Box in the dependent clauses in these sentences.

a. While you were out, someone called.

b. Although we were tired, we had fun.

c. They said that they were ready.

d. Let us know if you want to go with us.

e. After the sun set, the park closed for the day.

f. When you eat too much, swimming is not recommended.

III. Underline the verb in the main clause. Write "2" above this verb to indicate that it would be in second position in a German sentence.

a. Last night it snowed.

b. They really looked surprised.

c. With computers the work goes faster.

d. Tomorrow I have an appointment.

e. By the time we arrived, things were over.

f. In my German class last semester, we learned about the Berlin Wall.

WHAT ARE AFFIRMATIVE AND NEGATIVE SENTENCES? 40

A sentence, clause, or phrase can be classified according to whether it states a positive or negative fact.

Positive fact: The book is on the table.
Negative fact: The book is not on the table.

40.1 IN ENGLISH

Verbs in an affirmative sentence can be made negative in one of two ways:

- by adding *not* after auxiliary verbs or modals (Auxiliary verbs, p. 88)

Affirmative	**Negative**
Axel *is* a student.	Axel is *not* a student.
Jade *can* do it.	Jade can*not* do it.
They *will* travel.	They will *not* travel.

  The word *not* is often attached to the auxiliary and the letter "o" replaced by an apostrophe; this is called a **CONTRACTION**: is not → isn't; cannot → can't; will not → won't.

- by adding the auxiliary verb *do, does,* or *did* + *not* followed by the dictionary form of the main verb

Affirmative	**Negative**
We *study* a lot.	We *do not* study a lot.
Max *writes* well.	Max *does not* write well.
The train *arrived*.	The train *did not* arrive.

  The words *do, does, did* are often contracted with *not:* do not → don't; does not → doesn't; did not → didn't.

40.2 IN GERMAN

Unlike English, which always uses *not* to make an affirmative sentence negative, German uses either **nicht** (for verbs and other parts of speech) or **kein** (for specific nouns) depending on the part of speech being negated.

NICHT *(not)* → to negate verbs and other parts of speech. **Nicht** never changes form, but its position in the sentence varies:

- **Nicht** follows all personal pronouns, the subject, verb, direct object, and expressions of definite time.
- **Nicht** precedes everything else in the sentence.

Let's look at some examples.

40.2

Affirmative	**Negative**
Ich sehe dich.	Ich sehe dich **nicht.** personal pronoun + **nicht**
I see you.	*I **don't** see you.*
Er arbeitet in Berlin.	Er arbeitet **nicht** in Berlin. verb + **nicht** + prepositional phrase
He works in Berlin.	*He **doesn't** work in Berlin.*
Sie besucht Anna oft.	Sie besucht Anna **nicht** oft. direct object + **nicht** + adverb
She visits Anna often.	*She **doesn't** visit Anna often.*
Er kommt morgen Abend.	Er kommt morgen Abend **nicht.** definite time + **nicht**
He is coming tomorrow night.	*He is **not** coming tomorrow night.*

Your textbook will discuss the position of **nicht** in greater detail.

KEIN *(not a, not any, no)* → to negate a non-specific noun; i.e., a noun preceded by an indefinite article or no article.

- **Kein** agrees in case, gender, and number with the noun it precedes.
- **Kein** takes the same endings as indefinite articles (Articles, p. 26).

Let's look at some examples.

Affirmative	**Negative**
Anna sieht **einen** Hund. indefinite article *Anna sees **a** dog.*	Anna sieht **keinen Hund.** masc. sing. acc. (direct object) *Anna sees **no dog.*** *[Anna doesn't see a dog.]*
Ich habe Zeit. no article *I have time.*	Ich habe **keine Zeit.** fem. sing. acc. (direct object) *I have **no time.*** [*I don't have time.*]
Studenten wohnen hier. no article *Students live here.*	**Keine Studenten** wohnen hier. masc. pl. nom. (subject) ***No students** live here.*

Consult your textbook for more information on the usage of **nicht** and **kein.**

CAREFUL – Remember that in negative sentences in German there is no equivalent for the auxiliary verbs *do, does, did;* do not try to include them.

40.3 NEGATIVE WORDS

In both English and German there are other negative words besides *not* that can be added to an affirmative sentence.

IN ENGLISH

The most common negative words are *nothing, nobody, no one,* which can be used as subjects or objects of a sentence.

> *Nothing* is free.
> *Nobody* is going to the movies.
> subject
>
> I see *nothing*.
> I see *no one* (*nobody*).
> object

IN GERMAN

The most common negative words are **nichts** *(nothing)* and **niemand** *(no one, nobody)*. As in English they can be used as subjects or objects of a sentence.

- subject of the sentence

  > **Nichts** ist umsonst.
  > ***Nothing*** *is free.*
  >
  > **Niemand** geht ins Kino.
  > ***No one*** *is going to the movies.*

- object of the sentence — **nichts** doesn't change regardless of its function; **niemand** can be either in the masculine accusative **(-en)** or the masculine dative **(-em)** depending on the verb.

  > Ich sehe **nichts.**
  > *I see* ***nothing.***
  >
  > Ich sehe **niemanden.**
  > **sehen** *(to see)* takes an accusative object
  > *I see* ***no one.***
  >
  > Er hilft **niemandem.**
  > **helfen** *(to help)* takes dative object
  > *He helps* ***no one.***

CAREFUL – Note the spelling difference between **nicht** *(not)* and **nichts** *(nothing)*.

41 WHAT ARE DECLARATIVE AND INTERROGATIVE SENTENCES?

A sentence can be classified as to whether it is making a statement or asking a question.

A **DECLARATIVE SENTENCE** is a sentence that makes a statement.

> Franz arrived in Frankfurt at 11:15 a.m.

An **INTERROGATIVE SENTENCE** is a sentence that asks a question.

> Did Franz arrive in Frankfurt at 11:15 a.m?
> When did Franz arrive in Frankfurt?

In written language, an interrogative sentence always ends with a question mark.

41.1 IN ENGLISH

There are two types of interrogative sentences: questions that can be answered by "yes" or "no" and questions that ask for information.

YES-OR-NO QUESTIONS — Questions are formed from a declarative sentence in one of two ways:

- by adding the auxiliary verb *do, does,* or *did* before the subject + the dictionary form of the main verb.

Declarative sentence	**Interrogative sentence**
Ingrid *likes* the class.	*Does* Ingrid *like* the class?
Axel and Julia *sing* well.	*Do* Axel and Julia *sing* well?
Franz *went* to Berlin.	*Did* Franz *go* to Berlin?

- by inverting the normal word order of subject + verb to verb + subject. This **INVERSION** can only be used with auxiliary verbs or auxiliary words (Auxiliary verbs, p. 88).

Declarative sentence	**Interrogative sentence**
Franz is home. subject + verb *to be*	*Is* Franz home? verb + subject
You have received a letter. subject + *have* + main verb	*Have you received* a letter? *have* + subject + main verb
She will come tomorrow. subject + *will* + main verb	*Will she come* tomorrow? *will* + subject + main verb

ASKING FOR INFORMATION — Questions start with a question word, such as *when, who, which, and how,* + the interrogative sentence as formed above.

> *Why* does Julia like the class?
> *Where* did Ingrid go?

41.2 IN GERMAN

As in English, there are two types of interrogative sentences: yes-or-no questions and questions that ask for information with question words.

YES-OR-NO QUESTIONS — Questions are formed by the inversion process, i.e., by moving the conjugated verb from its second position in a declarative sentence to the first position and following it with the subject.

Declarative sentence	**Interrogative sentence**
Julia hat den Kurs gern. 1 subject + 2 conjugated verb ***Julia likes*** *the class.*	**Hat Julia** den Kurs gern? 1 conjugated verb + 2 subject ***Does Julia like*** *the class?*
Wir haben den Text schon gelesen. 1 conjugated verb + 2 subject ***We have*** *already read the text.*	**Haben wir** den Text schon gelesen? 1 conjugated verb + 2 subject ***Have we*** *already read the text?*

Exception: when a declarative sentence begins with a word other than the subject, the inversion process also occurs.

Morgen **kommt sie** wieder. 1 verb + 2 subject ***She is coming*** *again tomorrow.*	**Kommt sie** morgen wieder? 1 verb + 2 subject ***Is she coming*** *again tomorrow?*

ASKING FOR INFORMATION — Questions start with a question word, such as **wann** *(when)*, **wo** *(where)*, **warum** *(why)*, **wie oft** *(how often)*, + the interrogative sentence as formed above.

Warum hat Julia den Kurs gern?
Why *does Julia like the class?*

Wann kommt sie wieder?
When *is she coming again?*

CAREFUL — Remember that in interrogative sentences there is no equivalent for the auxiliary words *do, does, did* in German; do not try to include them.

41.3 TAG QUESTIONS

In both English and German when you expect a yes-or-no answer, you can also transform a statement into a question by adding a short phrase called a **TAG** at the end of the statement (see p. 158 "declarative").

IN ENGLISH

The tense of the statement dictates the tense of the tag and affirmative statements take negative tags and negative statements take affirmative tags (Chap. 40).

41.3

affirmative statement — negative tag

Axel and Ingrid *are* friends, *aren't they?*
(*are*: present; *aren't*: present)

Axel and Ingrid *were* friends, *weren't they?*
(*were*: past; *weren't*: past)

negative statement — affirmative tag

Axel and Ingrid *aren't* friends, *are they?*
(*aren't*: present; *are*: present)

Axel and Ingrid *weren't* friends, *were they?*
(*weren't*: past; *were*: past)

IN GERMAN

When confirmation is expected, the words **nicht wahr** or **oder** can be added to a statement. **Oder** can be used with either positive or negative statements, but **nicht wahr** is used only with affirmative statements.

negative statement

Du kommst heute nicht mit, **oder?**
You aren't coming along today, ***are you?***

affirmative statement

Sie wohnt in Berlin, **nicht wahr?**
She lives in Berlin, ***doesn't she?***

WHAT IS A CONJUNCTION? 42

A **CONJUNCTION** is a word that links two or more words or groups of words or clauses.

> He had to choose between good *and* evil.
> conjunction linking words
>
> They left *because* they were bored.
> conjunction linking clauses
>
> Let me know *when* you will arrive.
> conjunction linking clauses

42.1 IN ENGLISH

There are two kinds of conjunctions: coordinating and subordinating.

A **COORDINATING CONJUNCTION** joins words, phrases, i.e., groups of words without a verb, and clauses, i.e., groups of words with a verb, that are equal; it *coordinates* elements of equal rank. The major coordinating conjunctions are *and, but, or, nor, for,* and *yet.*

> good *or* evil
> word word
>
> over the river *and* through the woods
> phrase phrase
>
> They invited us *but* we couldn't go.
> clause clause

In the last example, each of the two clauses, "they invited us" and "we couldn't go," expresses a complete thought; therefore, each clause is a complete sentence that could stand alone. When a clause expresses a complete sentence it is called a **MAIN CLAUSE.** In the above sentence, the coordinating conjunction but links two main clauses (Sentence, p. 151).

A **SUBORDINATING CONJUNCTION** joins a main clause to a **DEPENDENT CLAUSE**; it *subordinates* one clause to another. A dependent clause does not express a complete thought; therefore, it is not a complete sentence. A clause introduced by a subordinating conjunction is called a **SUBORDINATE CLAUSE.** Typical subordinating conjunctions are *before, after, since, although, because, if, unless, so that, while, that,* and *when.*

In the following examples, the subordinate clauses are underlined, and the remaining words correspond to the main clause.

> *Although* we were invited, we didn't go.
>
> They left *because* they were bored.
>
> He said *that* he was tired.

Notice that the subordinate clauses may come either at the beginning of the sentence or after the main clause.

42.2 IN GERMAN

As in English, German has coordinating and subordinating conjuntions. Like adverbs and prepositions, conjunctions never change their form.

There are five coordinating conjunctions are **und** *(and)*, **oder** *(or)*, **aber** *(but)*, **denn** *(for)*, and **sondern** *(rather)*. Common subordinating conjunctions include **als** *(when)*, **weil** *(because)*, **wenn** *(if, whenever)*, **dass** *(that)*, **bevor** *(before)*, **während** *(while)*, and **nachdem** *(after)*.

It is important to recognize subordinating conjunctions because in German they affect the word order in the subordinate clause they introduce, as well as the word order in the main clause. As in English, the subordinate clause may come before or after the main clause.

- in the subordinate clause the conjugated verb is always placed at the end of the clause

  Ich fahre mit dem Bus, **weil** ich kein Auto **habe.**

  subordinating conjunction — verb at the end of the subordinate clause

  I go by bus ***because I have*** *no car.*

- if the subordinate clause comes at the beginning of the sentence, it functions as the first element in the sentence and the conjugated verb of the main clause is placed in the 2nd position, right after the conjugated verb of the subordinate clause, separated by a comma.

  1st position subordinate clause — 2nd position main clause

  Weil ich kein Auto **habe,** **fahre** ich mit dem Bus.

  conjugated verb — conjugated verb

  Because ***I have*** *no car,* ***I go*** *by bus.*

42.3 PREPOSITION OR CONJUNCTION?

IN ENGLISH

Some words function as both prepositions and subordinating conjunctions, for example, *before* and *after.* We can identify the word's function by determining whether or not it introduces a clause.

- if the word in question introduces a clause, i.e., a group of words with a verb, it is a subordinating conjunction.

  We left *before* the intermission began.
  sub. conj. subject + verb → clause

  After the concert was over, we ate ice cream.
  sub. conj. subject + verb → clause

- if the word in question is followed by an object, but no verb, it is a preposition.

  We left *before* the intermission.
  prep. object of preposition

  After the concert we ate ice cream.
  prep. object of preposition

IN GERMAN

It is important for you to establish whether a word is a preposition or a conjunction because in German you will use different words and apply different rules of grammar depending on the part of speech.

English	**German**	
Preposition and Conjunction	**Preposition**	**Conjunction**
before	vor	bevor
after	nach	nachdem

- *before* and *after* as conjunctions → **bevor** and **nachdem** connect two clauses and require two parts of speech, i.e., a subject and a verb.

  We left ***before*** *the intermission began.*
  subject + verb
  Wir sind weggegangen, **bevor** die Pause anfing.

  After *the concert was over, we ate ice cream.*
  subject + verb
  Nachdem das Konzert vorbei war, aßen wir Eis.

- *before* and *after* as prepositions → **vor** and **nach** are part of a phrase and require one part of speech, i.e., an object.

  We left ***before*** *the intermission.*
  object
  Wir sind **vor** der Pause weggegangen.

  After *the concert we ate ice cream.*
  object
  Nach dem Konzert haben wir Eis gegessen.

CAREFUL – To choose the correct German word and apply the appropriate rules of grammar, be sure to distinguish between a conjunction and a preposition: a conjunction introduces a clause and requires a subject and a verb, while a preposition requires only an object in a particular case.

STUDY TIPS
CONJUNCTIONS

Flashcard

1. Make a flashcard for each conjunction. On the English side, write the meaning of the conjunction. On the German side, write "coordinating" or "subordinating" and a sample sentence from your textbook.
2. Sort the flashcards into two categories: coordinating and subordinating. To remember the five cards in the coordinating pile: **sondern, oder, denn, aber, und,** use the acronym **SODAund.** All the other conjunctions belong in the subordinating category.

REVIEW ACTIVITY

I. Circle the coordinating and subordinating conjunctions.

a. We can have a picnic unless it starts raining.

b. She stopped studying because she was too tired.

c. He forgot his watch, but he remembered his passport.

d. Should we go out to eat or should we cook something at home?

II. Underline the prepositions in the following sentences. Box in the conjunctions.

a. Since the weather turned cold, we've stayed inside.

b. I've known him since high school.

c. We were home before midnight.

d. Before we leave, we'd better say goodbye.

WHAT IS AN ADVERB? 43

An **ADVERB** is a word that describes a verb, an adjective, or another adverb. It indicates manner, degree, time, place.

> Julia drives *well.*
> (drives = verb; well = adverb)
>
> The house is *very* big.
> (very = adverb; big = adjective)
>
> The girl ran *too quickly.*
> (too = adverb; quickly = adverb)

In English and in German, the structure for comparing adverbs is the same as the structure for comparing predicate adjectives (Adjectives, p. 116).

43.1 IN ENGLISH

There are different types of adverbs.

- an **ADVERB OF MANNER** answers the question *how?*

  Ingrid sings *beautifully.*

  Adverbs of manner are the most common and they are easy to recognize because they end with *-ly.*

- an **ADVERB OF DEGREE** answers the question *how much?*

  Axel did *well* on the exam.

- an **ADVERB OF TIME** answers the question *when?*

  He will come *soon.*

- an **ADVERB OF PLACE** answers the question *where?*

  The children were left *behind.*

A few adverbs in English are identical in form to the corresponding adjectives.

Adverb	**Adjective**
The guests came *late.*	We greeted the *late* guests.
Don't drive so *fast.*	*Fast* drivers cause accidents.
She works very *hard.*	This is *hard* work.

CAREFUL – Remember that in English *good* is an adjective since it modifies a noun and *well* is an adverb since it modifies a verb.

> The student writes *good* English.
> *Good* modifies the noun *English;* it is an adjective.
>
> The student writes *well.*
> *Well* modifies the verb *writes;* it is an adverb.

43.2 IN GERMAN

As in English, there are words that function only as adverbs.

> Das Haus ist **sehr** groß.
> *The house is **very** big.*
>
> Er kommt **bald**.
> *He is coming **soon.***

In German however, most adverbs, particularly adverbs of manner, have the same form as their corresponding adjective.

Adverb	**Adjective**
Du hast das **gut** gemacht.	Dieses Buch ist **gut.**
*You did that **well.***	*This book is **good.***
Sie singen **schön.**	Das Lied ist **schön.**
*They sing **beautifully.***	*The song is **beautiful.***
Wir fahren **schnell.**	Der Wagen ist **schnell.**
*We drive **fast.***	*The car is **fast.***

The most important fact for you to remember is that adverbs are invariable; i.e., unlike German adjectives they never change form.

CAREFUL – In English, the usual word order for adverbs is manner + place + time. In German, it is usually time + manner + place.

> *I am traveling by train to Munich **tomorrow.***
> (train = manner; to Munich = place; tomorrow = time)
>
> Ich fahre **morgen** mit dem Zug nach München.
> (morgen = time; Zug = manner; München = place)

Consult your textbook for the placement of adverbs.

STUDY TIPS
ADVERBS

Flashcard

Create flashcards for each German adverb you learn and its English equivalent. Note when it may be used as an adverb and adjective or only as an adverb.

früh	*early*	adjective & adverb
nie	*never*	adverb
langsam	*slow, slowly*	adjective, adverb

Another way of noting this difference is to use a dash (-) to mark words that are both adjectives and adverbs, because adjectives often require endings, and no (-) to mark words that are only adverbs which never take endings.

früh-	*early*
nie	*never*

REVIEW ACTIVITY

Circle the adverbs in the sentences below. Draw an arrow from each adverb to the word it modifies.

a. The guests arrived early.
b. They were too tired to go out.
c. David learned the lesson really quickly.
d. We stayed here.
e. Meg is a good student who speaks German very well.
f. The message was not clearly understood.

44 WHAT IS A RELATIVE PRONOUN?

A **RELATIVE PRONOUN** is a word used at the beginning of a clause that gives additional information about someone or something previously mentioned.

clause
additional information about *the book*

I'm reading the book *that* the teacher recommended.

A relative pronoun serves two purposes:

- as a pronoun it stands for a noun or an idea previously mentioned. The noun or idea to which it refers is called the **ANTECEDENT.**

  Here comes the boy *who* broke the window.
  antecedent of the relative pronoun *who*

  The weather was terrible, *which* ruined the picnic.
  this entire independent clause is the antecedent of the relative pronoun *which*

- it introduces a **SUBORDINATE CLAUSE**, also called a **DEPENDENT CLAUSE**; that is, a group of words having a subject and a verb that cannot stand alone because it does not express a complete thought. A subordinate clause is dependent on a **MAIN CLAUSE**; that is, another group of words having a subject and a verb that can stand alone as a complete sentence (Sentence, p. 149).

  (main clause: Here comes the boy) (subordinate clause: *who broke the* window.)
  verb: comes; subject: boy — subject: who; verb: broke

A subordinate clause that starts with a relative pronoun is also called a **RELATIVE CLAUSE.** In the example above, the relative clause starts with the relative pronoun *who* and gives us additional information about the antecedent *boy*.

Relative clauses are very common. We use them in everyday speech without giving much thought as to how we construct them. The relative pronoun allows us to combine two thoughts, which have a common element, into a single sentence. In this chapter, the relative clauses are underlined.

44.1 COMBINING SENTENCES WITH A RELATIVE PRONOUN

When sentences are combined with a relative pronoun, the relative pronoun can have different functions in the relative clause. It can be the subject, the direct object, the indirect object, or the object of a preposition.

Let us look at some examples of how sentences are combined.

- relative pronoun as a subject (Subject, p. 45).

  SENTENCE A The students passed the exam.
  SENTENCE B They studied.

1. **COMMON ELEMENT** – Identify the element sentences A and B have in common.

   Both *the students* and *they* refer to the same persons.

2. **ANTECEDENT** – The common element in sentence A will be the antecedent of the relative pronoun. The common element in sentence B will be replaced by a relative pronoun.

   The students is the antecedent. *They* will be replaced by a relative pronoun.

3. **FUNCTION** – The relative pronoun in the relative clause has the same function as the word it replaces.

   They is the subject of *studied.* It will be replaced by a subject relative pronoun.

4. **PERSON OR THING** – Identify whether the antecedent refers to a person(s) or a thing(s).

   The antecedent *students* refers to persons.

5. **SELECTION** – Choose the relative pronoun according to its function and its antecedent (steps 3 and 4 below).

   who

6. **RELATIVE CLAUSE** – Place the relative pronoun at the beginning of sentence B, thus forming a relative clause.

   who (that) studied

7. **PLACEMENT** – To combine the two clauses, place the relative clause right after its antecedent.

   The students <u>*who (that)* studied</u> passed the exam.

- relative pronoun as a direct object (Objects, p. 63)

  SENTENCE A This is the student.
  SENTENCE B I saw him.

  1. COMMON ELEMENT: *the student* and *him*
  2. ANTECEDENT: the student
  3. FUNCTION: *him* is the direct object
  4. PERSON OR THING: *the student* is a person
  5. SELECTION: *that* or *whom*
  6. RELATIVE CLAUSE: *that (whom)* I saw
  7. PLACEMENT: the student + *that (whom)*

  This is the student <u>*(that, whom)*</u> I saw.

- relative pronoun as an indirect object (Objects, p. 63)

    SENTENCE A This is the student.

    SENTENCE B I gave him advice.

    1. COMMON ELEMENT: *the student* and *him*
    2. ANTECEDENT: the student
    3. FUNCTION: *him* is the indirect object
    4. PERSON or thing: *the student* is a person
    5. SELECTION: *to whom*
    6. RELATIVE CLAUSE: *to whom* I gave advice
    7. PLACEMENT: the student + *to whom* I gave advice

    This is the student *to whom* I gave advice.

- relative pronoun as an object of a preposition (Prepositions, p. 80)

    SENTENCE A This is the student.

    SENTENCE B I spoke with him.

    1. COMMON ELEMENT: *the student* and *him*
    2. ANTECEDENT: the student
    3. FUNCTIONS: *him* is the object of the preposition *with*
    4. PERSON or thing: *the student* is a person
    5. SELECTION: *whom*
    6. RELATIVE CLAUSE: *with whom* I spoke
    7. PLACEMENT: the student + *with whom* I spoke

    This is the student *with whom* I spoke.

44.2 SELECTION OF A RELATIVE PRONOUN

IN ENGLISH

The selection of a relative pronoun in English depends not only on its function in the relative clause, but also on whether its antecedent is a "person" (human beings and animals) or a "thing" (objects and ideas). In standard and written English, *who* or *whom* are the relative pronouns used to refer to persons. In spoken English, they are often replaced by *that*. Moreover, in certain functions the relative pronoun is omitted altogether.

STANDARD: The teacher *(whom)* you wanted to see is not here.

SPOKEN: The teacher *(that)* you wanted to see is not here.

The distinction between spoken and standard English is important. In this chapter we refer to standard English which includes a relative pronoun.

IN GERMAN

Unlike English, the same set of relative pronouns is used for antecedents referring to persons and things and, more importantly, relative pronouns can never be omitted.

German relative pronouns are based on two factors:

1. GENDER AND NUMBER — the gender and number of the antecedent.
2. CASE FORM – their function in the relative clause

We shall look at each function separately. Notice that relative clauses are always separated by a comma from the main clause.

44.3 SUBJECT OF THE RELATIVE CLAUSE

IN ENGLISH

There are three relative pronouns that can be used as subjects of a relative clause, depending on whether the relative pronoun refers to a person or a thing. When it is the subject of a relative clause, the relative pronoun is never omitted.

PERSON — who (or that) → subject of the relative clause

She is the only student *who (that)* answered all the time.

THING — which or that → subject of the relative clause

The movie *which* is so popular was filmed in Germany.
The movie *that* is so popular was filmed in Germany.

Notice that the relative pronoun subject is always followed by a verb.

IN GERMAN

Relative pronouns that are the subject of the relative clause are in the nominative case. The form depends on the gender and number of the antecedent.

Singular		
Masculine	der	
Feminine	die	*who, that, which*
Neuter	das	
Plural	die	

To choose the correct form,

1. ANTECEDENT – Find the antecedent. (Don't forget that the antecedent is always the noun that precedes the relative pronoun.)
2. NUMBER & GENDER – Determine the number and gender of the antecedent.
3. SELECTION – Select the corresponding form in the nominative case.

Here is an example.

*The man **who** visited us was nice.*

1. ANTECEDENT: man
2. NUMBER & GENDER: **der Mann** *(the man)* is masculine singular
3. SELECTION: masculine singular nominative → **der**

Der Mann, **der** uns besuchte, war nett.

44.4 DIRECT OBJECT OF THE RELATIVE CLAUSE

IN ENGLISH

There are three relative pronouns that can be used as direct objects of a relative clause, depending on whether the relative pronoun refers to a person or a thing. Since relative pronouns are often omitted when they are objects of a relative clause, for reference we have indicated them in parentheses in the examples below in standard English.

PERSON — *whom* (or *that)* → object of a relative clause

- as a direct object

  This is the student *(whom, that)* I saw yesterday.

- as an indirect object

  Ingrid is the person *to whom* he gave the present.

THING — *which* (or *that)* → object of a relative clause

- as a direct object

  This is the book *(which)* Axel bought.

  This is the book *(that)* Axel bought.

- as an indirect object

  Here is the library *to which* he gave the book.

IN GERMAN

Relative pronouns that are the direct objects of the relative clause are either in the accusative or dative case, depending on the verb. The form used depends on the gender and number of the antecedent.

	Accusative	**Dative**	
Singular			
Masculine	den	dem	
Feminine	die	der	*who, that, which*
Neuter	das	dem	
Plural	die	denen	

Unlike English, relative pronouns are never omitted in German. (For reference, the equivalent English relative pronouns below are in parentheses.)

- as a direct object → accusative or dative

*Here is the student (**whom, that**) Franz saw last night.*

Hier ist der Student, **den** Franz gestern Abend sah.
masc. sing masc. sing. acc.

*The bag (**that**) I'm buying is expensive.*

Die Tasche, **die** ich kaufe, ist teuer.
fem. sing. fem. sing. acc. (**kaufen** takes an accusative object)

*The cat (**that**) the dog followed was black.*

Die Katze, **der** der Hund folgte, war schwarz.
fem. sing. fem. sing. dat. (**folgen** takes a dative object)

44.5 INDIRECT OBJECT OR OBJECT OF A PREPOSITION IN A RELATIVE CLAUSE

IN ENGLISH

Relative pronouns used as indirect objects or as objects of a preposition are the same as those used as direct objects. As is the case with other relative pronouns used as objects, they are often omitted. By integrating the preposition "to" before indirect objects and any other preposition within the sentence, you will be able to restore the relative pronoun.

Person — *whom* (or *that)* → indirect object or object of a preposition in a relative clause

Here is the student *(that) Franz gave the book **to.***
dangling preposition
Here is the student ***to whom** Franz gave the book.*

Ingrid is the person *(that) he went out **with.***
dangling preposition
Ingrid is the person ***with whom** he went out.*

Thing — *which* (or *that)* → object of a preposition in a relative clause

This is the library *that he was talking **about.***
dangling preposition
This is the library ***about which** I was talking.*

IN GERMAN

Relative pronouns that are the indirect objects take the dative case. Relative pronouns that are objects of a preposition take the case required by the preposition and reflect the gender of the antecedent. Since German places prepositions directly preceding their objects, you will need to restructure English phrases with dangling prepositions.

Here is the person (that) I was waiting ***for.*** →
Here is the person ***for whom*** *I was waiting.*
Hier ist die Person, **auf die** ich wartete.
fem. sing. fem. sing. **auf** + acc.

Here is the person (that) I was speaking ***with.*** →
Here is the person ***with whom*** *I was speaking.*
Hier ist die Person, **mit der** ich sprach.
fem. sing. fem. sing. **mit** + dat.

44.6 RELATIVE PRONOUN AS POSSESSIVE MODIFIER

IN ENGLISH

The possessive modifier *whose* does not change its form regardless of its function in the relative clause.

Here are the people *whose* car was stolen.
antecedent possessive modifying *car*

Look at the house *whose* roof was fixed.
antecedent possessive modifying *roof*

IN GERMAN

The possessive modifier is always in the genitive case. The form used depends on the gender of the antecedent.

Genitive			
Singular	Masculine	dessen	*whose*
	Feminine	deren	
	Neuter	dessen	
Plural		deren	

Let's look at an example.

*Hans, **whose** alarm clock was broken, overslept.*

1. ANTECEDENT: Hans
2. NUMBER & GENDER: *Hans* is masculine singular.
3. SELECTION: **dessen**

Hans, **dessen** Wecker kaputt war, hat sich verschlafen.

44.7 SUMMARY OF RELATIVE PRONOUNS

Here is a chart you can use as reference.

Function in relative clause	Antecedent singular			Antecedent plural
	Masculine	Feminine	Neuter	
Nominative	der	die	das	die
Accusative	den	die	das	die
Dative	dem	der	dem	denen
Genitive	dessen	deren	dessen	deren

44.8 RELATIVE PRONOUNS WITHOUT ANTECEDENT

There are relative pronouns that refer to an antecedent that has not been expressed or to an entire idea.

IN ENGLISH

The relative pronoun *which* can be used without an antecedent.

She didn't do well, *which* is too bad.
antecedent an idea: the fact that she didn't do well

IN GERMAN

There is also one relative pronoun that can be used without an antecedent: **was** *(which, what).*

Anna hat uns eingeladen, **was** wir nett gefunden haben.
*Anna invited us, **which** we found nice.*

Your textbook may give you examples of other instances that require the use of **was** as a relative pronoun.

STUDY TIPS
RELATIVE PRONOUNS

Pattern

To help you remember the forms of the relative pronouns, look for similarities with another part of speech such as definite articles.

Relative pronouns

	masc.	**fem.**	**neut.**	**pl.**
Nominative	der	die	das	die
Accusative	den	die	das	die
Dative	dem	der	dem	denen
Genitive	dessen	deren	dessen	deren

Definite articles

	masc.	**fem.**	**neut.**	**pl.**
Nominative	der	die	das	die
Accusative	den	die	das	die
Dative	dem	der	dem	den
Genitive	des	der	des	der

What are the similarities between relative pronouns and definite articles?

- nominative, accusative, and dative singular → identical
- genitive and dative plural → same first 3 letters **(des-, der-, des-, der-)**

Practice

Write two sentences that use the same noun in each sentence. Underline the noun, label its gender, and identify its function (case) in each sentence. Combine the two sentences, replacing one of the nouns with a relative pronoun. Pay attention to the case of the relative pronoun and the verb placement in the relative clause.

Der Bus ist spät.	der Bus: masc., subject → nom.
Ich warte auf **den Bus.**	den Bus: masc., direct object →acc.

Der Bus, auf **den** ich warte, ist spät.
The bus** is late. I'm waiting **for the bus. → ***The bus*** *(that) I'm waiting for* is late.

REVIEW ACTIVITY

I. Circle the antecedent of the relative pronoun in the following sentences.
Identify the function of the relative pronoun: subject (S), direct object (DO), indirect object (IO), object of a preposition (OP), possessive modifier (PM).

a. I received the letter that you sent me.	S	DO	IO	OP	PM
b. Those are the people who speak German.	S	DO	IO	OP	PM
c. The woman whom you met left today.	S	DO	IO	OP	PM
d. This is the book whose title I forgot.	S	DO	IO	OP	PM
e. Kit is the student about whom I spoke.	S	DO	IO	OP	PM
f. German is a language that about 130 million people speak.	S	DO	IO	OP	PM

II. The common elements in the sentence below have been highlighted. Fill in the information requested to find the correct relative pronoun and write a new English sentence using a relative pronoun.

a. The dog is friendly. It lives next door.

Function of element to replace: ____________________

Relative pronoun: ____________________

Combined sentence: ____________________

b. The Smiths left for Austria. You met them in Basel.

Function of element to replace: ____________________

Relative pronoun: ____________________

Combined sentence: ____________________

c. The new student is German. You were asking about her.

Function of element to replace: ____________________

Relative pronoun: ____________________

Combined sentence: ____________________

d. Andreas is my neighbor. His new car is parked outside.

Function of element to replace: ____________________

Relative pronoun: ____________________

Combined sentence: ____________________

45 WHAT IS MEANT BY MOOD?

MOOD in the grammatical sense refers to the forms of a verb that indicate the attitude of the speakers toward what they are saying: whether they are expressing a fact, a wish, an obligation, giving an order, etc.

Verb forms are divided into moods, which, in turn, are subdivided into one or more tenses. You will learn when to use the various moods as you learn verbs and their tenses. As a beginning student of German, you need to know the names of the moods so that you will understand what your textbook is referring to when it uses these terms.

45.1 IN ENGLISH

Verbs can be in one of three moods:

INDICATIVE MOOD — The indicative mood is used to indicate an action of the verb that really happens or is likely to happen. This is the most common mood, and most of the verb forms that you use in everyday conversation belong to the indicative mood. The indicative mood has a present tense (p. 60), a past tense (p. 102), and a future tense (p. 99).

> Hans *studies* German.
> Gabi *was* here.
> We *will go*.

IMPERATIVE MOOD — The imperative mood is used to express a command (p. 180). The imperative mood does not have different tenses.

> Hans, *study* German now!
> Anja, *be* here on time!

SUBJUNCTIVE MOOD — The subjunctive mood is used to express a subjective attitude or opinion about the action of the verb, a contrary-to-fact statement, or a wish (p. 183).

> The teacher recommended that Paul *do* the exercise.
> If she *were* here, we would go to the party.
> If only he *were* with us.

45.2 IN GERMAN

The same three moods exist and have their own special forms. As in English, the indicative is the most common mood; the imperative is used similarly in both languages; the subjunctive, which has a present and past tense, is used more frequently in German than in English. Refer to your textbook for the meaning and use of each form.

REVIEW ACTIVITY

Imagine how a speaker might say each sentence and indicate the mood of the verbs in italics: indicative (I), imperative (IM), or subjunctive (S).

a.	Columbus *discovered* America.	I	IM	S
b.	We wish you *were* here.	I	IM	S
c.	*Come* into the house, children!	I	IM	S
d.	We *have* bats in the attic.	I	IM	S
e.	*Look* at that!	I	IM	S
f.	If only I *had* more time!	I	IM	S

46 WHAT IS THE IMPERATIVE?

The **IMPERATIVE** is a verbal mood (p. 178) used to give someone an order, instructions, advice, or to make an offer. Since it does not have different tenses, adverbs of time can be added to indicate when the action should take place (Adverbs, p. 165).

> *Come* here [now]!
> *Arrive* early tomorrow!

46.1 IN ENGLISH

There are two types of commands, depending on who is told to do, or not to do, something.

"YOU" COMMAND — When an order is given to one or more persons, the dictionary form of the verb is used. The command can be softened by adding "please."

> *Answer* the phone.
> *Clean* your room.
>
> *Speak* softly.
> Please *close* the door.

"WE" COMMAND — When an order is given to oneself as well as to others, the phrase "let's" (a contraction of *let us*) is used + the dictionary form of the verb.

> *Let's leave.*
> *Let's go* to the movies.

The absence of the subject pronoun in the sentence is a good indication that you are dealing with an imperative and not a present tense.

> *You answer* the phone.
> present
>
> *Answer* the phone.
> imperative

46.2 IN GERMAN

As in English, there are two types of imperatives, depending on who is being told to do or not to do something.

"YOU" COMMAND — The *you*-command has three forms, corresponding to the three different personal pronouns for *you*: familiar **du, ihr,** and formal **Sie** (Personal pronouns, p. 41). The verb forms of the imperative are the same as the forms of the present tense indicative, except for the **du**-form. In written German an exclamation mark is used after an imperative.

- **DU-FORM** – When an order is given to a person to whom you say **du,** the imperative is formed by using the stem of the verb; some verbs can add the ending **-e,** but it is optional.

  Höre gut zu!
  Listen carefully.

  Höre!
  Listen.

  Schreib mir bald!
  Write *me soon.*

- **IHR-FORM** – When an order is given to two or more persons to whom you say **du** individually, the form of the verb is the same as the present tense indicative.

  Kommt mit!
  Come *along.*

  Esst nicht so schnell, Kinder!
  *Don't **eat** so fast, children.*

As in English, the subject pronoun is dropped in the **du** and **ihr** forms.

- **SIE-FORM** — When an order is given to one or more persons to whom you say **Sie** individually, the subject pronoun **Sie** is placed directly after the **Sie** form of the verb in the present tense. As in English, the command can be softened by adding **bitte** *(please).*

  Sprechen Sie lauter!
  Speak *more loudly.*

  Kommen Sie bitte mit!
  *Please **come** along.*

"WE" COMMAND — When an order is given to oneself as well as to others, the subject pronoun **wir** is placed directly after the **wir** form of the verb in the present tense.

Gehen wir jetzt!
Let's go *now.*

Sprechen wir Deutsch!
Let's speak *German.*

Your German textbook will explain in detail the rules for forming the imperative.

REVIEW ACTIVITY

Indicate the imperative form you would use when translating these sentences into German: du, ihr, Sie, or wir.

a.	Hurry up, Chris.	du	ihr	Sie	wir
b.	Let's go to the movies.	du	ihr	Sie	wir
c.	Close the door, children.	du	ihr	Sie	wir
d.	Excuse me a minute, Dr. Benn.	du	ihr	Sie	wir
e.	Please pick up your room, Ann.	du	ihr	Sie	wir
f.	Hurry up, everyone! (friends)	du	ihr	Sie	wir

WHAT IS THE SUBJUNCTIVE? 47

The **SUBJUNCTIVE** is a verb mood (Mood, p. 178) used to express hypothetical or contrary-to-fact situations, in contrast to the indicative mood that is used to express facts or likelihood.

> I wish Axel *were* here.
> hypothetical (Axel is not here) → subjunctive
>
> If Axel *were* here, you could meet him.
> contrary-to-fact (Axel is not here) → subjunctive
>
> Axel *is* here.
> fact (Axel is here) → indicative

47.1 IN ENGLISH

The subjunctive verb form can be is difficult to recognize because it is spelled like other tenses of the verb, the dictionary form and the simple past tense (Verbs, 29; Past tense, p. 102).

Indicative	Subjunctive
He *reads* a lot. indicative present *to read*	The course requires that he *read* a lot. subjunctive (same as dictionary form)
I *am* in Berlin right now. indicative present *to be*	I wish I *were* in Berlin. subjunctive (same as past tense but not for the 1st person singular)

In spoken English, the indicative form is sometimes used in place of the subjunctive, for example, *I wish I was there.*

The subjunctive occurs most commonly in three kinds of sentences.

- *if-clause* of contrary-to-fact sentences — the subjunctive form of the verb *to be (were)* is used. The result clause uses *would* + infinitive. The result clauses are underlined in the examples below.

  > If I *were* in Europe now, I would go to Berlin.
  > subjunctive in *if*-clause [contrary-to-fact: I am *not* in Europe]
  >
  > Franz would run faster, if he *were* in shape.
  > subjunctive in *if*-clause [contrary-to-fact: Franz is *not* in shape]

- conclusion of wish-statements — the subjunctive form of the verb *to be (were)* is used. The wish-statement is in the indicative.

  > I *wish* I *were* in Europe right now.
  > indicative subjunctive
  >
  > Franz *wishes* he *were* in shape.
  > indicative subjunctive

- following expressions that ask, urge, demand, request, or express necessity — the subjunctive form of any verb is used.

  She asked that I *come* to see her.
  request — subjunctive same as dictionary form

  It is necessary that he *study* a lot.
  demand — subjunctive same as dictionary form

47.2 IN GERMAN

As in English, German has two subjunctive forms: the **SUBJUNCTIVE II**, so called because the form is based on the second principal part of the verb, i.e., the simple past (Principal parts, p. 83), the most common subjunctive, is discussed in this chapter. The other, less common subjunctive, the **SUBJUNCTIVE I** (so called because the form is based on the first principal part of the verb, i.e., the infinitive) is discussed in (Discourse, p. 187).

The subjunctive II has a present and a past tense formed as follows:

PRESENT SUBJUNCTIVE II

The stem of the indicative past tense, **das Präteritum,** of the verb + subjunctive endings.

- **WEAK (REGULAR) VERBS** – the indicative past and the subjunctive II forms are identical.

  Infinitive: sagen *(to say)*
  Indicative past tense: sagte *(I said)*
  Past stem: sagt-

Indicative past	**Present subjunctive II**
Du **sagtest** . . .	Wenn du **sagtest** . . .
Er **sagte** . . .	Wenn er **sagte** . . .
*You **said** . . .*	*If you **were to say** . . .*
*He **said** . . .*	*If he **were to say** . . .*

- **IRREGULAR (STRONG) VERBS** – the stem vowels **a, o** and **u** of the indicative past add an umlaut. Note the addition of the letter **-e-** in the subjunctive endings.

  Infinitive: kommen *(to come)*
  Indicative past tense: kam *(I came)*
  Past stem (+ umlaut): käm- (p. 184)

Indicative past	**Present subjunctive II**	
ich kam	ich k**ä**m**e**	*I came, I would come*
du kam**st**	du k**ä**m**es**t	*you, etc.*
er kam	er k**ä**m**e**	
wir kam**en**	wir k**ä**m**en**	
ihr kam**t**	ihr k**ä**m**et**	
Sie kam**en**	Sie k**ä**m**en**	

PAST SUBJUNCTIVE II

The auxiliary verb **haben** *(to have)* or **sein** *(to be)* in the subjunctive II + the past participle of the main verb (Participles, p. 102).

Ich **hätte** das Buch **gekauft,** wenn ich es **gefunden hätte.**
past subjunctive — past subjunctive
I ***would have bought*** the book if I ***had found*** it.

Wenn wir nur früher **gekommen wären!**
past subjunctive
*If only we **had come** earlier!*

This tense is often used to talk about things in the past we wish we had done differently.

Consult your textbook for a detailed explanation of the subjunctive II forms, including exceptions.

THE WÜRDE-CONSTRUCTION

In spoken German, and increasingly in informal written German, the subjunctive II forms of the main verb are often replaced with the present subjunctive II form of **werden** *(to become)* + the infinitive of the main verb, a structure similar to the English structure *would* + the infinitive of the main verb.

ich **würde** kommen	*I **would** come*
du **würdest** kommen	*you **would** come*
er, sie, es **würde** kommen	*he, she, it **would** come*
wir **würden** kommen	*we **would** come*
ihr **würdet** kommen	*you **would** come*
sie, Sie **würden** kommen	*they, you **would** come*

The forms above have the same meaning as the subjunctive II forms: **ich käme, du kämest,** etc.

Let's look at two examples of the **würde**-construction.

> Ich **würde gehen,** wenn ich Zeit hätte.
> *I **would go** if I had time.*
>
> Sie **würden** dich **einladen,** wenn sie könnten.
> *They **would invite** you if they could.*

USAGE OF THE SUBJUNCTIVE II OR WÜRDE-CONSTRUCTION

The subjunctive II or the **würde**-construction is commonly used in three kinds of sentences.

- *if*-clause and result clause of contrary-to-fact sentences — Unlike English where the verb in the *if*-clause is in the subjunctive and the verb in the result clause uses *would* + infinitive, in German, the subjunctive II or **würde**-construction can be used in either or both clauses.

  *If she **were** here, I **would be** happy.*
  subjunctive *would* + infinitive
  Wenn sie hier **wäre,** dann **wäre** ich glücklich.
  subjunctive subjunctive

  *If it **were to rain,** I **would be** sad.*
  subjunctive + infinitive *would* + infinitive
  Wenn es **regnen würde,** dann **wäre** ich traurig.
  würde-construction subjunctive

- both clauses of wish-statements — Unlike English, where the verb in the wish-statement is in the indicative and subjunctive is only used in the conclusion of the wish-statement, in German, the subjunctive II is used in both the wish-statement and in the conclusion.

  *I **wish** she **were** here!*
  indicative subjunctive
  Ich **wünschte,** sie **wäre** doch hier!
  subjunctive subjunctive

  *She **wishes** she **had** more time!*
  indicative subjunctive
  Sie **wünschte,** sie **hätte** mehr Zeit!
  subjunctive subjunctive

- to form polite requests — Just as English uses the construction *would* or *could* + the infinitive to make polite requests, German uses the verbs **werden** *(to become)* and modals, such as **können** *(to be able to),* in the subjunctive II + the infinitive, and the formal *you*-form.

Could *you* ***do*** *me a favor?*
could infinitive
Könntest du mir einen Gefallen **tun?**
subjunctive infinitive

Would *you please* ***open*** *the door?*
would infinitive
Würden Sie bitte die Tür **aufmachen?**
subjunctive infinitive

- the auxiliary verbs **haben** *(to have)*, **sein** *(to be)*, and the modal verbs always use the one-word subjunctive II forms, and not the **würde**-construction (Auxiliary verbs, p. 87).

CAREFUL – Pay attention to the use of the umlaut in subjunctive II forms. It not only affects pronunciation, but completely changes the meaning of the sentence. Notice how the umlauted vowel can change the verb tense or mood.

Indicative past	**Subjunctive II**
Wir **waren gegangen.**	Wir **wären gegangen.**
We ***had*** *gone.*	*We* ***would have gone.***
Ich **konnte schwimmen.**	Ich **könnte schwimmen.**
I was able to swim.	***I would be able to swim.***

REVIEW ACTIVITY

Indicate whether each of the following statements is a statement of fact in the indicative (I) or a contrary-to-fact statement in the subjunctive (S).

a.	West Germany is approximately the size of Oregon.	I	S
b.	I wish I were finished already.	I	S
c.	If I had wings, I would fly away.	I	S
d.	Since things are going smoothly, we will be done soon.	I	S
e.	If they had come earlier, we could have gone for a walk.	I	S
f.	The rain is coming soon.	I	S

48 WHAT IS MEANT BY ACTIVE AND PASSIVE VOICE?

VOICE in the grammatical sense refers to the relationship between the verb and its subject. There are two voices, the **ACTIVE VOICE** and the **PASSIVE VOICE.**

ACTIVE VOICE — A sentence is said to be in the active voice when the subject is the performer of the action of the verb. In this instance, the verb is called an **ACTIVE VERB.**

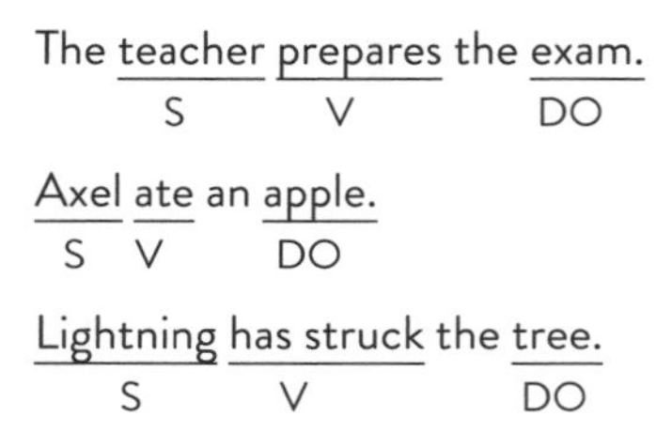

The teacher prepares the exam.
S V DO
Axel ate an apple.
S V DO
Lightning has struck the tree.
S V DO

In these examples the subject (S) performs the action of the verb (V) and the direct object (DO) is the receiver of the action (Subject, p. 45; Objects, p. 63).

PASSIVE VOICE — A sentence is said to be in the passive voice when the subject receives the action of the verb. In this instance, the verb is called a **PASSIVE VERB.**

The exam is prepared by the teacher.
S V agent

The apple was eaten by Axel.
S V agent

The tree has been struck by lightning.
S V agent

In these examples, the subject receives the action of the verb. The performer of the action, if it is mentioned, is introduced by the word "by" and is called the **AGENT.** When the agent is not mentioned, we do not know the performer of the action.

The lights were already turned on.
Since there is no agent, we don't know who performed the action of turning on the lights.

The passive voice is grammatically correct in English, but often avoided since the message is considered unclear. This is not the case in German where the passive is more common.

48.1 IN ENGLISH

The passive voice is expressed by the verb *to be* conjugated in the appropriate tense + the past participle of the main verb (Participles, p. 104). The tense of the passive sentence is indicated by the tense of the verb *to be*. The present passive is usually expressed by the present progressive tense *(is/are being)* rather than the present tense.

The exam *is being* prepared by the teacher.
present

The exam *was* prepared by the teacher.
past

The exam *will be* prepared by the teacher.
future

In English, only transitive verbs, i.e., verbs that can have a direct object, can be used in the passive voice.

MAKING AN ACTIVE SENTENCE PASSIVE

The steps to change an active sentence into a passive one are as follows.

1. The direct object of the active sentence becomes the subject of the passive sentence.

   Active The mechanic repairs *the car.* (direct object)

   Passive *The car* is repaired by the mechanic. (subject)

2. The tense of the verb of the active sentence is reflected in the tense of the verb *to be* in the passive sentence.

   Active The mechanic *repairs* the car. (present)

   Passive The car *is* repaired by the mechanic. (present)

   Active The mechanic *has repaired* the car. (present perfect)

   Passive The car *has been* repaired by the mechanic. (present perfect)

3. The subject of the active sentence becomes the agent of the passive sentence or the agent is omitted.

   Active *The mechanic* is repairing the car. (subject)

   Passive The car is being repaired *by the mechanic.* (agent)

   The car is being repaired. [no agent]

48.2 IN GERMAN

The passive voice is formed by the verb **werden** *(to become)* conjugated in the appropriate tense + the past participle of the main verb.

Der Roman **wird** gelesen.
present + past participle (**lesen**) → infinitive passive
*The novel **is being** read.*

Der Roman **wurde** gelesen.
simple past + past participle (**lesen**) → infinitive passive
*The novel **was (being)** read.*

Der Roman **wird** gelesen **werden.**
future + past participle (**lesen**) → infinitive passive
*The novel **will be** read.*

Note that in the passive future tense there are two forms of **werden**, one conjugated + the infinitive to mark the future tense (p. 99) and one as part of an infinitive phrase, i.e., the past participle + **werden** in the infinitive, to mark the passive voice.

Der Roman **ist** gelesen **worden.**
perfect
*The novel **was (has been)** read.*

Der Roman **war** gelesen **worden.**
past perfect
*The novel **had been** read.*

As you can see in the last two examples, in passive sentences the perfect and past perfect tenses drop the **ge-** of the past participle of **werden: geworden** → **worden.**

MAKING AN ACTIVE SENTENCE PASSIVE

To change an active sentence into passive in German, follow the same steps as for English. The form of **werden** must agree in number with the new subject. The tense of passive sentence is indicated by the tense of the verb **werden**. You will also have to change the case of the words to reflect their new function in the passive sentence.

Subject — The accusative object of an active sentence becomes the nominative subject of the passive sentence.

Active *The woman reads **the novel.***
Die Frau liest **den Roman.**
accusative

Passive ***The novel** is read by the woman.*
Der Roman wird von der Frau gelesen.
nominative

Active *Ilse sings **such songs.***
Ilse singt **solche Lieder.**
accusative

Passive ***Such songs** are sung by Ilse.*
Solche Lieder werden von Ilse gesungen.
nominative

Agent — If the agent is mentioned, it is expressed differently depending on whether it refers to a person or not.

- **Person** – If the nominative subject of an active sentence is a person, it is expressed by **von** + dative object in a passive sentence.

Active	***Many people*** *heard the speech.* **Viele Leute** hörten die Rede. nominative
Passive	*The speech was heard* ***by many people.*** Die Rede wurde **von vielen Leuten** gehört. **von** + dative

- **Not a person** – If the nominative subject of an active sentence is not a person, it is usually expressed by **durch** + accusative object in a passive sentence.

Active	***Fire*** *has destroyed the building.* **Feuer** hat das Gebäude zerstört. nominative
Passive	*The building was destroyed* ***by fire.*** Das Gebäude ist **durch Feuer** zerstört worden. **durch** + accusative

Like in English, an instrumental agent with **mit** (with) is also possible.

Das Bild wurde **mit** einem Stift gezeichnet.
The picture was drawn ***with*** *a pen.*

IMPERSONAL PASSIVES

Unlike English where only transitive verbs can be used in the passive voice, German sometimes uses intransitive verbs, verbs that cannot have a direct object, in the passive voice. Such constructions are called **IMPERSONAL PASSIVES** because the verb expresses an activity with no reference to a personal subject. The emphasis is on the activity, rather than on who is doing it. In place of a personal subject, the impersonal pronoun **es** is introduced as the formal subject of the sentence. The auxiliary **werden** is conjugated to agree with **es.**

Active	Die Angestellten **sprechen** Deutsch. *The employees* ***speak*** *German.*
Passive	**Es wird** hier Deutsch **gesprochen.** *German* ***is spoken*** *here.* [word-for-word: it is here German spoken]

48.2

If you change a sentence whose verb takes a dative object from active to passive, the dative object remains in the dative case instead of becoming the subject of the passive sentence. If the impersonal subject **es** is added, the word order has to be changed so that the conjugated verb is in the second position.

Active	Man dankt **ihm.** dative object *One thanks **him.***
Passive	**Ihm** wird gedankt. **Es** wird **ihm** gedankt. dative subject ***He** is thanked.*
Active	Sie glaubten **den Kindern** nicht. dative object *They didn't believe **the children.***
Passive	**Den Kindern** wurde nicht geglaubt. **Es** wurde **den Kindern** nicht geglaubt. dative subject ***The children** were not believed.*

Note that many impersonal passives in German cannot be translated word-for-word into English. Your textbook will show you several alternatives to the passive construction in German.

REVIEW ACTIVITY

I. Underline the subject in the following sentences.

i. Circle the performer of the action.

ii. Identify each sentence as active **(A)** or passive **(P).**

a. The cow jumped over the moon.	A	P
b. The game was cut short by rain.	A	P
c. They camped by the river.	A	P
d. This film will be enjoyed by everyone.	A	P

II. Underline the verb in the following sentences.

i. Identify the tense of each sentences: past **(PA),** present **(P),** future **(F).**

ii. Keeping the same tense, rewrite the sentence in the passive voice on the line provided.

a. The parents dropped off the children.	PA	P	F
b. Work crews are clearing the road.	PA	P	F
c. People all over the world will see this program.	PA	P	F
d. Shakespeare wrote the play in 1597.	PA	P	F

a. ______________________________

b. ______________________________

c. ______________________________

d. ______________________________

49 WHAT IS MEANT BY DIRECT AND INDIRECT DISCOURSE?

DIRECT DISCOURSE refers to a statement made directly between a speaker and a listener. Direct discourse is usually set in quotation marks.

> Inge said, "I am going to Berlin."
> Axel asked, "What will you do in Berlin?"

INDIRECT (REPORTED) DISCOURSE refers to another person's statement which is reported.

> Inge said she was going to Berlin.
> Axel asked what she would do in Berlin.

While indirect discourse reproduces the substance of the message, it cannot reproduce the statement word-for-word. Some words, such as pronouns and possessive adjectives, must be changed to reflect the change of speaker.

49.1 IN ENGLISH

When direct discourse is changed to indirect discourse there is a shift in tense in the reported speech to situate the action in relation to when the speaker reports it.

Direct discourse
Inge said, "*I am going* to Berlin."
PRONOUNS: I → she
TENSE: am going (present) → was going (past)
Indirect discourse
Inge said *she was going* to Berlin.

Direct discourse
Inge said, "*I was* in Berlin with *my* sister."
PRONOUNS: I → she
POSSESSIVE ADJECTIVE: my → her
TENSE: was (past) → had been (past perfect)
Indirect discourse
Inge said *she had been* in Berlin with *her* sister.

49.2 IN GERMAN

Unlike English where there is only a shift in tense when changing direct to indirect discourse, in German there is also a shift in mood (Mood, p. 178). In direct discourse the verb is in the indicative, in indirect discourse the verb is in the **SUBJUNCTIVE I.**

The subjunctive I, so called because it is based on the 1st principal part of the verb, i.e., the infinitive, has a present and a past tense. The same forms are used for weak and strong verbs (Principal parts, p. 83).

Present subjunctive I → the stem of the infinitive + the subjunctive endings. The vowel changes in the 1st and 2nd person singular of stem-changing verbs do not apply.

Infinitive: fahren *(to drive)*

Stem: fahr-

Indicative present	**Present subjunctive I**
ich fahr**e**	ich fahr**e**
du fähr**st**	du f**ahrest**
er fäh**rt**	er f**ahre**
wir fahr**en**	wir fahr**en**
ihr fahr**t**	ihr fahr**et**
Sie fahr**en**	Sie fahr**en**

Here is an example:

Direct discourse

Ingrid sagte, "Ich **fahre** nach Berlin."
present indicative

*Ingrid said, "I **am going** to Berlin."*
Pronoun: I (**ich**) → she (**sie**)
Mood: I am going (**ich fahre** — indicative) →
she was going (**sie fahre** — subjunctive I)

Indirect discourse

Ingrid sagte, sie **fahre** nach Berlin.
subjunctive I present

*Ingrid said she **was going** to Berlin.*

Past subjunctive I → the subjunctive I form of the helping verb **haben** *(to have)* or **sein** *(to be)* + the past participle of the main verb.

Direct discourse

Ingrid sagte, "Ich **war** in Berlin."
simple past indicative

*Ingrid said, "I **was** in Berlin."*
Pronoun: I (**ich**) → she (**sie**)
Mood: I was (**ich war** — indicative) →
she had been (**sei gewesen** — subjunctive I)

Indirect discourse

Ingrid sagte, sie **sei** in Berlin **gewesen.**
subjunctive I past

*Ingrid said she **had been** in Berlin.*

In German, the indicative mood and the two subjunctive forms can be used to distinguish the speaker's attitude toward reported information. Consider the following sentence:

Er sagt, er ist klug.
Er sagt, er sei klug.
Er sagt, er wäre klug.
He says he is clever.

In the first example, the use of the indicative suggests that the person reporting the speech agrees with what is said; in the second, the use of the subjunctive I suggests neutral reporting; and in the third, the use of the subjunctive II casts doubt on the truth of what is said.

The subjunctive I is used primarily in written and news reporting, but is increasingly intermingled with the subjunctive II (Subjunctive II, p. 177), which is used in casual conversation. Your German textbook will explain the use of the subjunctive in indirect discourse in greater detail.

REVIEW ACTIVITY

Underline the verbs in the quotations below.

i. Indicate whether the verb describes an action in the present (P) or in the past (PA).
ii. Box in any pronouns or possessive adjectives within the quotation that will change when these sentences are in indirect discourse.
iii. Rewrite these direct discourse sentences as indirect discourse.

a. She asked, "How is the weather?" P PA
She asked ____________________

b. They shouted, "We found the trail." P PA
They shouted that ____________________

c. He announced, "I just got my driver's license." P PA
He announced that ____________________

d. Libby said, "I'm coming." P PA
Libby said that ____________________

e. Tony called out, "I'm done." P PA
Tony called out that ____________________

f. The researchers stated, "our estimate is 50% growth." P PA
The researchers stated that ____________________

2. **WHAT IS A NOUN?**

a. Katie, teacher, questions, Europe **b.** Mrs. Schneider, students, patience **c.** curiosity, part, learning **d.** Katie, classmates, stories, Berlin, capital, Germany **e**. class, exhibit, settlers **f.** German, countries, parts, Luxembourg

3. **WHAT ARE PREFIXES AND SUFFIXES?**

I: **a.** de- **b**. en- **c.** mis- **d**. re- **e**. pre- **f.** per-
II: **a.** -ency **b.** -ful **c.** -less **d.** -ly **e.** -ness **f.** -able

4. **WHAT IS MEANT BY NUMBER?**

I: **a.** plural **b.** singular **c.** singular **d**. plural **e.** singular **f.** singular **g.** singular **h.** plural
II: **a.** ö + -er **b**. ü + -e **c**. -er **d.** -nen **e.** -s **f.** ä **g.** -en **h.** no change

5. **WHAT IS MEANT BY GENDER?**

a. M **b.** N **c.** F **d.** M **e.** F **f.** N **g.** F **h.** M

6. **WHAT IS AN ARTICLE?**

a. das **b.** ein **c.** eine **d.** das **e.** ein **f.** die **g.** der **h.** der

7. **WHAT IS A VERB?**

I: **a.** meet **b.** eat **c.** stayed, expected **d.** took, finished, went **e.** felt, talked **f.** drives, arrives
II: **a.** teach **b.** be **c.** have **d.** leave **e.** swim **f.** find

9. **WHAT IS A PRONOUN?**

The antecedent is between parentheses: **a.** she (Brooke) **b.** they (Molly and Stan) **c.** it (chair) **d.** herself (Sara) **e.** her (Helga) **f.** it (the Second World War)

12. **WHAT IS A SUBJECT PRONOUN?**

a. Q: Who goes? A: I (Singular) **b.** Q: Who are? A: My brother and sister (Plural) **c.** Q: Who doesn't work? A: They (Plural) **d.** Q: Who has to work? A: I (Singular)

13. **WHAT IS A PREDICATE NOUN?**

The subject is between parentheses: **a.** news (letter) **b.** doctor (Carol) **c.** tourists (they) **d.** musician (Dan) **e.** place (pool) **f.** challenge (situation)

14. **WHAT IS A VERB CONJUGATION?**

I: **a.** denk- **b.** renn- **c.** arbeit- **d.** wander- **e.** reis- **f.** tu- **g.** vertret- (with stem change) **h.** mitnehm- (separable, with stem change)
II: **a.** Stem: geh-; gehe, gehst, geht, gehen, geht, gehen **b.** Stem: lauf- (with stem change); laufe, läufst, läuft, laufen, lauft, laufen

16. WHAT IS THE PRESENT TENSE?

a. do play **b.** plays **c.** is playing **d.** are playing **e.** do play

17. WHAT IS AN OBJECT?

a. A: my homework (DO) **b.** A: a postcard (DO) A: her friend (IO) **c.** A: my brother (IO) A: those books (DO)

18. WHAT ARE DIRECT AND INDIRECT OBJECT PRONOUNS?

a. 2nd, singular **b.** 3rd, singular **c.** 3rd, singular **d.** 3rd, plural

19. WHAT IS A PREPOSITION?

I: **a.** behind **b.** under **c.** at, in **d.** on, around **e.** at **f.** without. II: **a.** I can't tell about what they're laughing. **b.** For whom are you doing that? **c.** At what place does he work? **d.** That's not some thing in which I am interested.

20. WHAT IS AN OBJECT OF PREPOSITION PRONOUN?

Nouns referring to persons are in italics: **a.** *Greg*, preposition + pronoun **b.** present, **da**-compound **c.** *Emily*, preposition + pronoun **d.** *vacation*, **da**-compound **e.** situation, **da**-compound **f.** *classmates*, preposition + pronoun

21. WHAT ARE THE PRINCIPAL PARTS OF A VERB?

a. W **b.** S **c.** M **d.** S **e.** W **f.** S **g.** M **h.** W

22. WHAT IS AN AUXILIARY VERB?

The auxiliary verbs and modals are in parentheses; the English auxiliaries that will not be expressed are in italics; the verbs that will be expressed in German are outside the parentheses: **a.** (*are* working) working **b.** (can go) can go **c.** (*do* have) have **d.** (has waited) has waited **e.** (will arrive) will arrive **f.** (shall do) shall do

23. WHAT ARE REFLEXIVE PRONOUNS AND VERBS?

I: **a.** yourself **b.** ourselves **c.** himself **d.** herself **e.** myself **f.** your selves
II: mich, dich, sich, uns, euch, sich

24. WHAT IS THE FUTURE TENSE?

a. are going → present **b.** will go → future **c.** shall return → future **d.** am flying → present **e.** 's coming → present **f.** will return → future

25. WHAT IS THE PAST TENSE?

I: **a.** went (SP) **b.** has visited (PP) **c.** was (SP) **d.** travelled (SP) **e.** have shown (PP) **f.** have seen (PP)

26. WHAT IS A PARTICIPLE?

I: **a.** watching (P) **b.** gone (PP) **c.** broken (PP) **d.** studying (P) **e.** prying (P) **f.** sunk (PP)

30. WHAT IS A DESCRIPTIVE ADJECTIVE?

I: The noun or pronoun described is between parentheses: **a.** red (door) AE **b.** fresh (juice) AD **c.** old (shoes) NA **d.** large (pizza) AD, **e.** friendly (face) AE **f.** green (grass) NA

31. WHAT IS MEANT BY COMPARISON OF ADJECTIVES?

a. The teacher is older than the students. **b.** This student is as intelligent as that one. **c.** Kathy is less tall than Molly. **d.** This movie is the best this season. **e.** Today is the hottest day on record. **f.** That is more interesting than what I heard about it yesterday!

32. WHAT IS THE POSSESSIVE?

I: The possessor is in italics: **a.** the motors of the cars **b.** the end of the year **c.** the works of Bachmann **d.** the name of the street **e.** the museums of Berlin **f.** the introduction of the book

33. WHAT IS A POSSESSIVE ADJECTIVE?

I: The possessive adjective is in italics:
a. their exams **b.** her coat, her scarf **c.** his comb, his pocket
d. my backpack, my room

34. WHAT IS A POSSESSIVE PRONOUN?

a. yours **b.** ours **c.** hers **d.** his **e.** mine

35. WHAT IS AN INTERROGATIVE ADJECTIVE?

I: The interrogative adjective is in italics: **a.** what newspaper
b. which record **c.** what homework **d.** which hotel **e.** which game **f.** what car
II: **a.** About which topic did you write? **b.** To which people did you talk?

36. WHAT IS AN INTERROGATIVE PRONOUN?

a. who, person, subject → wer
b. what, thing, direct object → was **c.** whose, person, possessive → wessen
d. who (for whom), person, object of preposition → wen

37. WHAT IS A DEMONSTRATIVE ADJECTIVE?

The modified noun is in parentheses: **a.** every (room) **b.** this (house) **c.** all (houses) **d.** these (windows) **e.** those (closets)

39. WHAT IS A SENTENCE?

I: **a.** to do your best (IP) **b.** Before the play (PrP) **c.** at the last minute (PrP) **d.** to start early (IP), **e.** organizing her room (PP) **f.** listening to loud music (PP)

ANSWER KEY

II: **a.** While you were out **b.** Although we were tired **c.** that they were ready **d.** if you want to go with us **e.** After the sun set **f.** When you eat too much
III: **a.** snowed **b.** looked **c.** goes **d.** have **e.** were **f.** learned

42. WHAT IS A CONJUNCTION?

I: **a.** unless **b.** because **c.** but **d.** or
II: **a.** since (c) **b.** since (p) **c.** before (p) **d.** before (c)

43. WHAT IS AN ADVERB?

The word modified is after the comma: **a.** early, arrived **b.** too, tired **c.** really, quickly, learned **d.** here, stayed **e.** very, well, speaks **f.** clearly, understood

44. WHAT IS A RELATIVE PRONOUN?

The antecedent is in italics:
I: **a.** *letter*, that → DO **b.** *people*, who → S **c.** *woman*, whom → DO **d.** *book*, whose → PM **e.** *student*, whom → OP **f.** *language*, that → DO
II: **a.** S, that; The dog that lives next door is friendly.
b. DO, whom; The Smiths, whom you met in Basel, left for Austria.
c. OP, whom; the new student, about whom you asked, is German.
d. S, whose; Andreas, whose new car is parked outside, is my neighbor.

45. WHAT IS MEANT BY MOOD?

a. indicative **b.** subjunctive **c.** imperative **d.** indicative **e.** imperative **f.** subjunctive

46. WHAT IS THE IMPERATIVE?

a. du **b.** wir **c.** ihr **d.** Sie **e.** du **f.** ihr

47. WHAT IS THE SUBJUNCTIVE?

a. I **b.** S **c.** S **d.** I **e.** S **f.** I

48. WHAT IS MEANT BY ACTIVE AND PASSIVE VOICE?

I: The subject is followed by the performer of the action in italics:
a. cow, cow → A **b.** game, rain → P **c.** they, they → A **d.** film, everyone → P
II: **a.** dropped (PA) → The children were dropped off by the parents. **b.** are clearing (P) → The road is being cleared by work crews. **c.** will see (F) → This program will be seen by people all over the world. **d.** wrote (PA) → The play was written by Shakespeare in 1597.

49. WHAT IS MEANT BY DIRECT AND INDIRECT DISCOURSE?

a. P, . . .how the weather was. **b.** PA, [We], . . .they had found the trail. **c.** PA, [I, my], . . .he had just gotten his driver's license. **d.** P, [I], . . .she was coming. **e.** P, [I] . . .he was done. **f.** P, [our] . . .their estimate was 50% growth.

INDEX